Sovereign Debt Sustainability

In 2020, the G20 proposed a solution for the debt-related issues affecting the world's poorest countries due to the COVID-19 pandemic. However, their initiatives have failed to meet their objectives. The author argues that the reason for this failure is the inability to bring sovereign countries to the table to re-negotiate their debt agreements with private creditors as they fear credit rating agencies and the prospect of a downgrade. The author refers to this as the 'credit rating impasse'.

This book proposes a novel solution. The author asserts that there is a need in the literature to unpick the dynamic that exists and creates that impasse, namely the pressures that exist between sovereign states, private creditors, credit rating agencies, and the geo-political backdrop that is massively influential in the dynamic, that is, the adversarial relationship between China and the US.

This book addresses the recent history of debt treatment for poorer countries and related successes and failures: COVID-19-related issues and the development of the Debt Service Suspension Initiative and the Common Framework for Debt Treatment. This book examines the reasons for their failure by analysing the positions of the sovereign states, the division between private and official creditors and between multilateral institutions such as the IMF and the World Bank, credit rating agencies, and the competing political entities of China and the US. It presents a wider picture of the systemic underpinnings to such debt-related issues and, when examined through a geo-political perspective, the subsequent chances of future debt treatment-related successes.

Daniel Cash is a Senior Lecturer at Aston University, UK, a Fulbright Scholar at New York University's Stern Business School, and specialises in the regulation of the credit and ESG rating agencies.

Routledge International Studies in Money and Banking

Mergers, Acquisitions, and International Financial Regulation
Analysing Special Purpose Acquisition Companies
Daniele D'Alvia

Pension Fund Capitalism
The Privatization of Pensions in Developed and Developing Countries
Leokadia Oręziak

Central Banks in Organizational Networks
Entangled Market Actors
Christoph F-D. Wu

Responsible Finance and Digitalization
Implications and Developments
Edited by Panu Kalmi, Tommi Auvinen and Marko Järvenpää

Digital Currencies and the New Global Financial System
Edited by Ranjan Aneja and Robert Dygas

Negative Interest Rates and Financial Stability
Lessons in Systemic Risk
Karol Rogowicz and Małgorzata Iwanicz-Drozdowska

Digital Finance and the Future of the Global Financial System
Disruption and Innovation in Financial Services
Edited by Lech Gąsiorkiewicz and Jan Monkiewicz

Sovereign Debt Sustainability
Multilateral Debt Treatment and the Credit Rating Impasse
Daniel Cash

For more information about this series, please visit: www.routledge.com/Routledge-International-Studies-in-Money-and-Banking/book-series/SE0403

Sovereign Debt Sustainability

Multilateral Debt Treatment and the Credit Rating Impasse

Daniel Cash

Routledge
Taylor & Francis Group
LONDON AND NEW YORK

First published 2023
by Routledge
4 Park Square, Milton Park, Abingdon, Oxon OX14 4RN

and by Routledge
605 Third Avenue, New York, NY 10158

Routledge is an imprint of the Taylor & Francis Group, an informa business

British Library Cataloguing-in-Publication Data
A catalogue record for this book is available from the British Library

Library of Congress Cataloging-in-Publication Data
Names: Cash, Daniel (Law teacher), author.
Title: Sovereign debt sustainability : multilateral debt treatment and the credit rating impasse / Daniel Cash.
Description: Milton Park, Abingdon, Oxon ; New York, NY : Routledge, 2023. | Includes bibliographical references and index.
Identifiers: LCCN 2022028183 (print) | LCCN 2022028184 (ebook) | ISBN 9781032198651 (hardback) | ISBN 9781032198668 (paperback) | ISBN 9781003261223 (ebook)
Subjects: LCSH: Credit ratings—Developing countries. | Debt—Developing countries. | Developing countries—Economic conditions—21st century. | Economic development—Developing countries.
Classification: LCC HG3751.9.D44 C37 2023 (print) | LCC HG3751.9.D44 (ebook) | DDC 332.709172/4—dc23/eng/20220630
LC record available at https://lccn.loc.gov/2022028183
LC ebook record available at https://lccn.loc.gov/2022028184

ISBN: 978-1-032-19865-1 (hbk)
ISBN: 978-1-032-19866-8 (pbk)
ISBN: 978-1-003-26122-3 (ebk)

DOI: 10.4324/9781003261223

Typeset in Bembo
by Apex CoVantage, LLC

Contents

Preface

No country has managed to escape the COVID-19 pandemic, with even the most isolated parts unable to avoid the pain and suffering that the pandemic has brought with it. However, that pain and suffering, whether physical, mental, social, or economic, is not shared equally. Whilst developed regions have had the ability to take luxury safeguarding positions like 'furlough' strategies, direct payments for missed employment, excessive vaccination drives, and publicly supporting whole industries, large amounts of the global population have suffered the brunt of the virus. Large parts of South America, Central America, Asia, and Africa have been left without access to vaccinations, placed on travel ban lists, and lost vital parts of their economies as the world 'locked down'.

For a variety of reasons, countries that already had unstable economies were immediately pushed into a state of panic and worry. A large majority of developing countries are heavily dependent on loans and external financing to meet their societal and economic needs and, overnight, the ability to meet those external financing needs was turned on its head. Cut off from usual financial flows, a number of countries were immediately faced with a tragic proposition: invest in one's healthcare infrastructure to fend off the tragic effects of the pandemic or continue to service the array of loans that would still be due to be paid, regardless of the pandemic. For many countries, the reality was much more nuanced, but essentially those same countries were faced with a binary choice. Multilateral institutions such as the International Monetary Fund, the World Bank, and the G20 stepped into this space with a programme that would allow debts to be restructured so that the savings for the countries could be instead invested into the healthcare infrastructures. At the same time, the World Health Organisation was pleading for a global response to help defeat the pandemic. 'Official' creditors lined up, and in the early stages of the Debt Service Suspension Initiative (DSSI), more than $5 billion was saved through restructurings (via deferrals, not cancellations). However, this was less than predicted. 'Private' creditors, such as institutional investors, did not participate, and the result was that savings from 'official' restructurings merely went into servicing 'private' debt.

However, this dynamic only affected those that signed up for the DSSI; many did not. It seems strange that a country would not sign up for an initiative designed to relieve its debt burden, and even more so when we consider that the initiative that followed – the *Common Framework* – was even less popular. The reason? The credit rating agencies. The credit rating agencies made abundantly clear that if a country were to join an initiative that pushed for equivalence in debt treatment, that is, that any restructuring deal must be concluded with private creditors also, then the agencies would see this as a potential default event and would, in turn, send the country's rating into default. The effect of this, in theory, is that returning to the investment categories so that private creditors would continue to lend would be very difficult. The threat of being locked out of the capital markets has essentially led to the international initiatives failing.

This book charts this dynamic and focuses, majoritively, on Africa. It does so because the majority of those eligible, and those who have engaged with such international initiatives, are on the African continent. In telling the story, this book tells of a continent that has had a particular history with 'debt', and of a continent that has historically, and which continues to today, been at the centre of global pressures. In adjoining that analysis to a demonstration of what I call the 'credit rating impasse', this book concludes with proposals on how the impasse can be breached. Sometimes it is difficult to relate financial mechanisms to human realities like death or deprivation, but here the link is clear: without the resources to fight the pandemic, the citizenry of said countries are and will continue to be in grave danger.

Acknowledgements

I would like to sincerely thank the Open Societies Foundation (OSF) for their funding that made possible the project this book relates to. Their support extended far beyond funding, providing me with access to world-leading experts with whom I spoke to at length, as part of roundtables and on a personal basis; their help with sharing their network with me was invaluable. The ideas and comments in this book, however, do not necessarily represent the views and position of the OSF – all the work and associated errors are mine alone.

As part of the Credit Rating Research Initiative (CRRI) project that the OSF supported, I would also like to thank my home institution, Aston University, for supporting me in my endeavours and for helping host the CRRI as it continues to grow in its nascent stages.

The CRRI project brought in a number of academic partners, to whom I am grateful. I am particularly grateful to the team at Credit Rating Analytics led by Saveshen Pillay. Saveshen and the team produced fantastic work for the project which, by itself, has majorly inspired me to write this book. I must also thank Saveshen for introducing me to a unique, inspiring, and influential African perspective that has also shaped my views on these issues. Meeting with and listening to different people who are pushing to positively affect the global imbalance that appears to centre on the African continent has been a personal pleasure, and I hope to capture the sentiments of our conversations and my learning in this work.

Introduction

> *Today's global financial system is supercharging inequalities and instability. It is a system that allows credit rating agencies to undermine the credibility of developing countries with good growth prospects and vital development needs, and this obviously makes private finance become more risk averse.*[1]

Though the global warning system for public health emergencies was triggered very early in the life of the COVID-19 virus, very few heeded the warnings.[2] What followed was a once-in-a-generation pandemic that would go on to affect every part of the world. Aside from the truly devastating and tragic loss and injury that the pandemic has caused, one of the clearest results has been that the pandemic has shone a light on deeply rooted, often historical, but wholly systemic inequalities on the global scene. Whilst some countries have been able to 'lock down' and utilise their resources to compensate their citizenry for loss of earnings, other countries have been brutally exposed to the harshness of the pandemic. Furthermore, some countries have been able to provide for up to four doses of COVID-19 vaccines, whilst some have such low levels of vaccination coverage with single-digit percentages of citizens even having had their first vaccine, that such statistics start to become painfully irrelevant. Vaccine inequality has become a microcosm of the general inequality witnessed on a global scale.

For this book, what has been done to help those vulnerable countries being exposed to the pandemic is of concern. This is for two reasons. On one side, the attempts to help reveal oft-overlooked prejudices and systemic inequality; usually, these elements are intertwined in some of the most ruthless and inhumane histories the planet has ever known. On the other side, the attempts to help allow us to examine the technical aspects of a global system that keeps producing the same results, irrespective of the form taken. In the extract used for the opening comment above, the UN Secretary-General states that *today's* global financial system is supercharging inequalities and instability, but this book will question that position – not because Antonio Guterres is wrong in his sentiment, but because to suggest it is just today's financial system that is causing such problems overlooks systemic patterns that go back much further than the current iteration of the financial system.

DOI: 10.4324/9781003261223-1

To do this, we could begin anywhere in truth. The financial system is made up of a myriad of components that could be accused of supercharging inequality and instability. The negative relationship between the Global North and the Global South in terms of perpetuating inequality and instability is a long and storied one. We will be focusing on one particular dynamic: the *credit rating dynamic*. I will repeat this term throughout the book, and by it, I mean a particular relationship that exists between a sovereign state, credit rating agencies, multilateral institutions and their members (including non-affiliated bilateral partners, in acknowledging the lack of unity at the global level), and private creditors who are predominantly made up of large 'institutional' investors. The pandemic has revealed that when it comes to global finance that affects whole countries, this particular dynamic is arguably the most important. Short of war to underpin a global financial system affecting countries, it is these identified players that make up the particular machine that we will be focusing on.

At this early point in the proceedings, it is likely important to speak very simplistically. This book is concerned with what I call the 'credit rating impasse' and overcoming it. To spell that concept out, we need to start with the concept of sovereign debt. Kim Oosterlinck provides us with an excellent first foray into the concept when she tells us that, simply, 'sovereign debts are the debts issued by a sovereign government', although 'despite its apparent simplicity, this definition hides a complex reality'.[3] The complex reality lies not in the actual technicalities of issuing debt that others can invest in for a return, but in the duality of the contract itself; more specifically, the relationship between the borrower and the bondholder, which is not static. The concept of a sovereign state borrowing and promising to pay with a premium is not a modern one, and according to Oosterlinck, it can be traced back to antiquity. She notes that large-scale borrowing seems to have emerged from the 15th century onwards, and since that time, the constitution of a stereotypical bondholder has changed from private wealthy individuals and families and banks, then other countries which caused severe international issues, then investment banks, and now, majoritively, to private creditors usually consisting of some of the world's largest investment vehicles (alongside banking institutions and other sovereigns).[4] There is a slow march towards a new phase of sovereign debt ownership, and understanding, acknowledging, and remembering that progression is very important for us in this book.

Whilst acknowledging the position of the creditor is vital, one must also consider the position of the debtor because all are not created equal in the eyes of the financial system. As we shall see in Chapter 1, there is no recognised international court of justice to oversee the intricate web of global sovereign bonds and, thus, no site of arbitration or negotiation. There is no global bankruptcy court. As Oosterlinck explains:

> In comparison to debts issued by corporations, the reimbursement of sovereign debts is thus much harder to enforce. This difficulty stems from the immunity that sovereigns enjoy. In the past, sovereigns benefited from

> an absolute immunity: they could not be sued and their assets could not be seized. Nowadays, a more restrictive form of immunity prevails. The United States has indeed allowed private claimants to sue foreign governments. Commercial assets could thus, in theory, be seized, even if this is not necessarily easy to implement.[5]

With this immunity in mind and the lack of a formal bankruptcy structure, the global financial system has utilised different means to allow capital to flow or not flow as the case may be. This brings us to the target of the book: the credit rating agencies. Traditionally, agents examined and opined on the creditworthiness of commercial debt; however, the role of credit rating agencies has grown and developed over the past six or seven decades – now they effectively stand as the gatekeepers[6] for debt issued by corporates, sovereigns, municipals, and a wide array of financial products. In addition, *how* they rate is theoretically changing, with the leading agencies beginning to consider the effects of non-financial aspects such as climate in a more coordinated and systemic manner (as they argue). Moreover, the crucial addition of advisory services specialising in several related fields[7] and the alternative chosen, as opposed to developing a global bankruptcy vehicle, is clear to see. With the push by bilateral creditors (countries) and multilateral lenders (e.g. the World Bank and the International Monetary Fund [IMF]) to entice more private creditors into the equation to lessen the need for themselves to provide support and potentially lose money, the role of the credit rating agencies has become more pronounced. For a variety of reasons, private creditors depend on the ratings that the credit rating agencies produce.

We will certainly be returning to this point later in the book, but an important question to ask of the last sentence above is 'why?' Why is it that private creditors rely on the credit rating agencies? There are many possible answers to this question; however, there is, unfortunately, no one right answer. The answer depends on how one analyses the rating industry. For example, one argument is that a private investor would utilise the ratings because of duplicity costs; if an investor was to undertake the necessary research into every investment opportunity themselves, the margin to make money from the opportunity would be so low, or non-existent, that the global investment machine would grind to a halt immediately. Therefore, the presence of a third party to perform that research is preferable. Although before the late 1960s, credit rating agencies charged investors for the rating information (at a palatable cost for investors of the time), the fact that now it is the issuers of debt that pay for the ratings means that for investors, there is no actual cost to utilising the rating information. That relationship between the issuer and the rating agency also now means that the rating agencies have access to corporate/sovereign information that, via its alphanumeric rating system, they can project to the marketplace without compromising the commercial sensitivity of the information the issuer has provided, resulting in richer information on the issuer and its creditworthiness. Thus, the cost may be a factor. However, after the Financial Crisis, when the credit rating agencies were shown to be conspiring with the issuers of toxic debt, legislation across the world pushed for investors to consider other sources of creditworthiness assessment, all to no avail. Though investors are no longer forced by legislative and regulatory rules to use ratings, their usage has increased since, as evidenced by the record revenues being recorded by the largest rating agencies. The rating agencies were shown to be acting *against* investors, yet their usage has not decreased since but rather gone from strength to strength. There must be a reason for this.

This is where I have developed the concept of a 'signalling theory' applicable to this dynamic.[8] Signalling theory, when applied in this context, is based on a very simple and universal constant: the concept of *trust*. For example, if I were to tell you that I, myself, could be trusted to repay a loan on time from you, why would you have any reason to believe me? You may be inclined to believe me because of an aspect that you value – perhaps one's reputation, for example – but the question then becomes whether your trust in that value system is enough to convince you to part with your resources. This is the first test, and you can see why just trusting in my word may not be enough, irrespective of my reputation (whatever that may be). That responsibility would also be heightened massively if you were not only investing your own resources in the loan to me but that of several other people too. This next test makes things even more difficult because now you are risking the resources of other people too; one's word becomes increasingly difficult to trust when your responsibilities are increased. Let us extrapolate this further and place you in a professional role managing the resources of others, with that role being attached to several professional and legal responsibilities that could see you in great professional and personal danger if you make the wrong decision. Now the issue of trust has vanished, and one's word or reputation is simply not enough. With all that considered, such professional roles demand that you invest the collected resources somewhere to make returns on those collected resources. This is where the need to signal becomes pertinent.

In the above scenario, the issuer of the debt (the entity asking for investment) needs to convince the entity with the resources that they can be trusted. What is needed, per the market reality, is an independent third party that majoritively has the constraining feature of maintaining its reputation to opine on the trustworthiness of the issuer. If we adjoin to this the concept of information asymmetry, which means that one party fundamentally knows more about a certain element than the opposing party, then the presence of the third party is crucial.[9] This is just one element of the signalling theory's application to this dynamic because, in truth, it applies to every constituent of the dynamic: issuers need to signal to investors; investors of the sophisticated kind need to signal to their principals with whose resources they are investing; principals within investment vehicles may need to constrain the actions of their agents by attaching recognised and, perhaps, easy-to-understand standards to the mandates of those directing agents; market participants need to signal to regulators that they are acting in accordance with norms; and regulators need to signal to market participants what standards need to be met. The credit ratings, when we consider the capital markets, stand at the epicentre of this signalling dynamic.

In this digression on the utility of credit ratings, you may be asking yourself how is it that credit rating agencies sit on such a fundamental throne which requires one to be independent when it is the issuers of debt who are paying for the ratings. Why would investors in debt choose to trust an entity that is so clearly in a compromised position? In the late 1960s in the US, the largest rating agencies switched their remuneration model from investor-pays to issuer-pays. There are several reasons as to why they did this, but all are disputed. Some argue that technological advances in the field of photocopying forced their hands, and the investment world just accepted the switch.[10] Others have suggested that the institutional reliance on the ratings developed by the SEC in 1973 allowed the rating agencies to change their model with impunity,[11] though we can dismiss this suggestion purely on the basis that the agencies began changing their model in the late 1960s, first with municipal debt and then with everything else. However, it is through the lens of signalling theory that I argue we reveal the truth of why investors would accept compromised third parties. Historical research[12] has shown that rating agencies, in their various guises (from credit reference companies to credit rating companies [a close lineage is visible upon inspection]), have always been 'relied' upon and also protected from various official entities, ranging from the courts to the securities regulators. However, the dominant theory regarding the major turning point for the success of the modern rating agencies – the 1970s – is that credit rating agencies were mostly irrelevant and close to collapsing. I have argued elsewhere that the real reason credit rating agencies miraculously became fundamental overnight was not because of the accepted reasons in the literature but because of the collapse of the Penn Central Railroad Company in the early 1970s which left many investors holding now-worthless investments that were all top-rated by a company called the National Credit Office.[13] The dominant third party for creditworthiness assessments at the time, mainly because of its penchant for providing top ratings to securities that they had very little idea about in a time of Post-War hubris, the National Credit Office had decimated its reputation via the collapse of the Railroad Company, and investors hurriedly ran to an alternative. The almost academic-focused rating agencies (then) were who they ran to, and the rating agencies, on top of all of the factors, changed their remuneration model to take advantage of their new position in the eyes of investors and issuers who needed to convince them.

I have included the above to give you a short and sharp insight into what a credit rating agency is. It is relevant for us because of the concept of a 'rating impasse'. Though not intended to forego the analysis coming later, but now that we know why the rating agencies sit at the centre of the dynamic described earlier consisting of sovereign issuers and majoritively private investors who do not have a bankruptcy procedure to rely upon, understanding the concept of a multilateral debt initiative brings everything together.

In the next chapter, we will go through the modern history of debt treatment concerning the African continent; the reasons for the focus on Africa and its history will be made clear shortly. There are two debt initiatives in particular that we will focus on because they are the global order's response to the pandemic, namely the Debt Service Suspension Initiative (the DSSI) and the initiative that followed, namely the Common Framework for Debt Treatments Beyond the DSSI, or Common Framework as it is colloquially known. Both were set up by the G20, with the World Bank and the IMF administering particular elements of the initiatives. First came the DSSI, with the aim of postponing service payments of the debts of the world's most vulnerable countries (not just African countries, but African countries made up a large proportion of those eligible). This was supposed to save those countries nearly $12 billion over a short period, with the aim being to then allow those countries to distribute their savings into their overwhelmed health and social infrastructures. I say 'supposed' because that did not happen. What did happen is that there was an instant divergence in who participated because not even all of the eligible 'official' creditors took part (an 'official' creditor is another country or multilateral institution, e.g. the World Bank). The World Bank said that it could not participate due to having to protect its resources to continue to provide support, whilst major official creditors such as China decided to strike their own deals on debt treatment owing to their considerable economic presence in the regions affected. Meanwhile, the private creditors did nothing. Holding a large proportion of outstanding debt, the request for voluntary participation from private creditors went unheard. Private creditors complained via their collective institutions such as the Institute of International Finance (IIF) that they needed the debtor countries to come forward under the scheme and none had. But why would the countries so desperately in need not come forward for help? Here is where the credit rating agencies come into play.

The credit rating agencies, recognised as not being proactive on behalf of investors in the Financial Crisis, were now making themselves very clear. Any country that even sought to initiate any proceedings that *could* lead to a private investor losing money would immediately be deemed to be a default risk with the likelihood, so the leading rating agencies said and continue to affirm, being that the country would be rated as being in default and, thus, lose their access to the capital markets. Some have argued that countries should not be put off by this and that it would be financially healthier for them, in the long run, to default.[14] However, it is also the case that the credit rating agencies have been running their own concerted campaign to push the narrative that fighting default is the best way forward, and it appears that the countries have listened. Few countries joined the DSSI because of this fear of being rated as in default; as such, the initiative was deemed unsuccessful. As the Common Framework takes over the work of the DSSI, the same problem persists with no end in sight: countries paralysed by fear developed by the credit rating agencies and, as we shall see, the private investors as well. This, in this book and in every other work on the subject, is what I call the 'credit rating impasse'.

That is the focus of this book. However, the 'target' is Africa, and for good reason. African countries make up the majority of those deemed eligible for the two multilateral initiatives. This is the foremost reason for the book's focus on the continent. In addition, Africa has a unique history with the 'global order', and the current dynamic, in many ways, is symptomatic of a long-held prejudice directed towards the continent; as the former president of Burkina Faso said in 1987, 'Debt is neo-colonialism'.[15] Colonialism is a vital part of this whole story; therefore, we shall be assessing, in a targeted way, that important concept shortly in the book. However, whilst I may use the word 'Africa' throughout the book, this is not because I do not acknowledge the vast and extraordinary diversity on the continent. In a continent that could separately house Europe, the US, India, and China and have plenty of room to spare, there is no one 'Africa' of course. As Boulle et al. rightly note:

> At the same time it is dangerous to treat Africa, as many external commentators do, as a single economic entity. It is of course a continent of approximately one billion people with extensive diversity in relation to culture, politics and economies such that few generalisations can be made in respect of some regions, let alone the continent as a whole. The continent is sometimes seen from two divides: sub-Saharan Africa, generally encompassing countries lying south of the Sahara Desert; and Arab North-Africa, referring to countries lying north of the Sahara. Ironically the relative lack of infrastructure, including basic roads and other forms of transport, within parts of the continent not only renders trade difficult to manage among African states themselves but also excludes the harmonising influences of enhanced economic activity across borders.[16]

Thus, it is with the greatest of respect and humility that I will use the term 'Africa' to refer to the collective countries on the continent though not all are eligible for entry into the multilateral initiatives; although it is worth noting that with the analysis we will undertake in this book, it is clear that, systemically, all countries in the region are suspectable to becoming victim to the financial system as it is designed.

It is likely appropriate to move into the book at this stage, but there is an important aspect to remember before we do. This book will aim to provide some ideas as to how to navigate the 'credit rating impasse'. It will provide details of the debt treatment history for the region and how it impacted the region's development. The book will then analyse the impact of the pandemic upon the region, and then detail every element of the credit rating impasse, before concluding with ideas on how to navigate it for the benefit of the citizens of the region. It is this point that I would like to emphasise before we begin. There is often a disconnect between the failures or fundamental problems within a given financial system and the effects on human beings, but in this example, we have a clear connection: the actions of financial players are leaving human beings without, left to face the extraordinary harshness of a global pandemic alone and without adequate protection. Whilst some countries are planning for their citizens to have their *fourth* dose, the vast majority of people in our region of focus have not had their first. This is simply not right on a humanist level. Something needs to be done and there is an important reason why; we must not forget those who need to be helped, in a purely humanistic manner, in this situation. I leave this introduction with a quote from Chris Jochnick and Fraser Preston as they say it much better than I ever could:

> Setting aside the periodic crises and stunted development caused by over-indebtedness, the real cost of sovereign debt is paid in tiny instalments every day by people without access to health care, education, and clean water, whose livelihoods are crimped by crumbling public infrastructure and faltering economies.[17]

Notes

1 Antonio Guterres, 'Opening Remarks at Secretary-General's End-of-year Press Encounter' (2021) *United Nations* (Dec 16) www.un.org/sg/en/node/261243.
2 Amy Maxmen, 'Why Did the World's Pandemic Warning System Fail When COVID Hit?' (2021) *Nature* (Jan 23) www.nature.com/articles/d41586-021-00162-4.
3 Kim Oosterlinck, 'The Historical Context of Sovereign Debt' in Illias Bantekas and Cephas Lumina, *Sovereign Debt and Human Rights* (OUP 2019) 13.
4 Ibid.
5 Ibid.
6 John C. Coffee, *Gatekeepers: The Professions and Corporate Governance* (OUP 2006).
7 The ancillary services 'race' is as hot as it has ever been in the credit rating field, with the top agencies spending tens of billions to acquire companies that can accentuate their already-substantial service offerings . . . for a price. For more on the effect of this side development to the underlying function of providing impartial and unbiased ratings for investors to use, see Daniel Cash, *Regulation and the Credit Rating Agencies: Restraining Ancillary Services* (Routledge 2018).
8 For a description of this theory, see Chapter 4.3 in Daniel Cash, *Sustainability Rating Agencies vs Credit Rating Agencies: The Battle to Serve the Mainstream Investor* (Palgrave Macmillan 2021).
9 Marguerite Mendell and Erica Barbosa, 'Impact Investing: A Preliminary Analysis of Emergent Primary and Secondary Exchange Platforms' (2012) 3 *Journal of Sustainable Finance & Investment* 2 111–123, 113.
10 Eva H. Wirten, *No Trespassing: Authorship, Intellectual Property Rights, and the Boundaries of Globalisation* (The University of Toronto Press 2004) 61.
11 Frank Partnoy, 'The Paradox of Credit Ratings' in Richard M. Levich, Giovanni Majnoni, and Carmen Reinhart, *Ratings, Rating Agencies and the Global Financial System* (Kluwar 2002) 70–72.
12 Predominantly the fantastic works of Marc Flandreau and his students:
13 See Cash (n 7) Chapter 3.3.1.1.
14 Moritz Kraemer, 'Bondholders Need to Forgive Some African Debt' (2020) *Financial Times* (Aug 27) www.ft.com/content/7d93235c-ffea-44bc-a0f0-fa1de09012b3.
15 Joan Chaker, *Debt as Colonialism* (Progressive International 2021).
16 Laurence Boulle, Emmanuel T. Laryea, and Franziska Sucker, 'International Economic Law and African Development – An Introduction' in Laurence Boulle, *International Economic Law and African Development* (Siber Ink 2014) 6.
17 Chris Jochnick and Fraser A. Preston, 'Introduction' in Chris Jochnick and Fraser A. Preston, *Sovereign Debt at the Crossroads: Challenges and Proposals for Resolving the Third World Debt Crisis* (OUP 2006) 3.

1 A Modern History of Debt Treatment for African Countries

1.1 Introduction

It would be more than appropriate at this early stage in the book to provide a chronological analysis of Africa's history with the modern concept of debt. However, the current pandemic and how Africa has been forced to deal with it is symptomatic of a much deeper relationship that is historic and continues to be negatively impactful. That history, which we shall touch upon shortly, is a lens with which we must analyse the current situation on the continent. Whilst the concept of colonialism may make for uncomfortable reading, it is a vital aspect of the story we are discussing here. It is for this reason that we shall now try to understand the concept of colonialism in the African context some more; only then can the small number of meaningful and theoretically impactful debt treatment initiatives be discussed. This will provide us with the basis to see the current-day debt treatment initiatives in the correct light.

There will be a direct focus on four particular elements of debt treatment with the continent in mind. The four instances will provide us with an insight into what was considered appropriate, how those initiatives worked in practice, and why some debt treatment initiatives were considered to be inappropriate for the debt dynamic affecting vulnerable sovereign states. This will be helpful because it will set out for us, rightly or wrongly, what may be acceptable on the global stage. This is not to say that grand and ambitious ideas and projects are not worthy (quite the opposite) because as Anne Krueger once wrote: '[some] questions will not be easy to answer. But it is important not to shy away from the challenge'.[1] Yet, if we consider the practical arguments that defend the status quo in this instance and the wide array of large and influential players involved, then pragmatism may arguably be the best way forward; it is more likely that pragmatic amendments to the current system will be more palatable to the industry figures and entities involved.

However, it is arguably time to change the narrative. Empowered nation states dictating the terms of their aid for such a dire situation and ultimately continuing a ruinous and vicious circle of debt dependency must end. In this chapter, we will see many debt treatment initiatives that arguably have colonialism at their heart and a genuine desire to help but only in so much that an

DOI: 10.4324/9781003261223-2

element of debt dependency is preserved. Hopefully, the narrative surrounding debt treatment can be made sufficiently clear so that you, as the reader, can see the lineage between the shocking history that the continent has endured in the relatively modern era and the underlying aims of the debt treatment initiatives, which by virtue of the continent now being offered new debt treatment initiatives in the DSSI and the Common Framework surely means that previous initiatives have failed. It must surely mean that they have failed if we consider that their aims were to eradicate debt dependency; however, as we shall see, that is not necessarily the case.

1.2 The Colonialist Foundation

The first thing to note is that this is not a book about the horrors of the colonial conquests that devastated the African continent; there are many enlightening books on the subject that provide us with tremendous insight into that chapter in human history.[2] The aim is not to provide an encyclopaedic account, but to present aspects that can inform our narrative as we seek to dissect the modern debt treatment initiatives. For instance, we shall start with the onset of what is known as the Slave Trade, although the pre-colonial relationship that was dominated by the European sea-fairing nations also fits this transactional narrative between continents, as Rodney affirms:

> The first significant thing about the internationalisation of trade in the fifteenth century was that Europeans took the initiative and went to other parts of the world. No Chinese boats reached Europe, and if any African canoes reached the Americas (as is sometimes maintained), they did not establish two-way links. What was called international trade was nothing but the extension overseas of European interests. The strategy behind international trade and the production that supported it was firmly in European hands, and specifically in the hands of the sea-going nations from the North Sea to the Mediterranean. They owned and directed the great majority of the world's sea-going vessels, and they controlled the financing of the trade between four continents. Africans had little clue as to the tri-continental links between Africa, Europe, and the Americas. Europe has a monopoly of knowledge about the international exchange system seen as a whole, for Western Europe was the only sector capable of viewing the system as a whole.[3]

What is described above is, essentially, informational asymmetry in action. On the back of that advantage, European nations began replacing majoritively Arab trading routes between Africa and India and utilised their militaristic advantage to control more of the African continent. By the mid-1500s, a large number of the West and East coasts of the African continent could be described as 'economic satellites'.[4] On this basis, the European Slave Trade that followed may be seen as an almost economic endeavour, particularly with the usage of the term 'trade'. Yet, this is simply not the case because whilst human beings were 'traded' from the inner parts of the continent to the coastal regions, often being bought and resold along the way, how those human beings were put in that position had no economic background as they were brought into this 'trade' through 'warfare, trickery, banditry, and kidnaping'.[5] Whilst some Western scholars have put forward the argument that the slave trade was a *moral* evil but not an *economic* evil based on the fact that *some* Africans profited from the trade and this 'wealth' could then be distributed, we can easily dismiss these arguments.[6] What is not debatable is that the slave trade, inclusive of the Western- and Eastern-facing campaigns, brought powerful nations to the African continent in a concerted way, so much so in fact that the continent soon became a contested landscape between nations scrambling to acquire lucrative resources.[7]

There have been explanations put forward – admittedly, Eurocentric ones – as to why there was such a scramble to carve up the African continent like a cake for the devourment of Europeans. Amongst the main protagonists were the British, the French, the Germans, the Portuguese, and the Spanish, along with King Leopold II of Belgium who would hold the heart of the continent with the most brutalist of grips. Hobson suggested that surplus capital within Europe led to the scramble for more profit, whilst others have argued that the sub-imperialist nature of Africa at the time created fertile ground. However, there is no agreement on the driving forces of the crusade.[8] What is clearer is that the infighting that blighted the European continent for centuries was transplanted to the African continent with many 'internal' wars taking place, such as the Boer War. However, that thirst for more territory and the 'lottery' of natural resource extraction would force the European nations to revert to militaristic colonialism, rather than the diplomatic religion-based colonialism that early endeavours had favoured. The level of loss and brutality was unheard of in modern history, and it would not be forgotten.

The details and impact of the colonial surge on the continent is important to recognise. As we are concerned with debt and the treatment of it, we can 'fast-forward' to the time of general independence, when former European colonies were granted their 'freedom' from their European masters. However, the suffering incurred tells us, perhaps, two sides of the same coin in relation to 'independence'. On the one side, the vicious history African people endured would have been sure to have been at the forefront of their minds when building their new nations. On the other, the psychology of a. being connected to such endeavours and b. profiting so handsomely from it surely affects the leaving conquerors. To be able to conduct oneself in such a manner means there must have been reasoning that would allow one to act so inhumanly, and such theories and understandings were in ready supply for the Europeans.[9] This is pertinent because such ideologies are difficult to replace or even lessen, having utilised them for so long. This is an extremely important aspect to remember when we look at the African experience post-Independence.

1.3 The Post-Independence Landscape

The 1960s predominantly, as well as the 1970s, represent an apparent change in the African landscape as many countries won independence. However, it has been said that 'their independence was and in most cases remains more apparent than real'.[10] Whilst many African countries became independent before the 1960s and 1970s (12 to be exact),[11] 1960 alone saw 17 and the period between 1960 and 1979 saw 44 countries in total gain their independence.[12] However, we need to be careful with such figures because the reality is much different. As Mwakikagile describes:

> When most African countries won independence in the sixties, the former colonial powers wanted to maintain close ties with their former colonies for a number of reasons: economic control; political domination; strategic interests; Cold War imperatives; and national prestige. They still considered their former colonies as their property. Colonialism was transmuted into neocolonialism but in essence it remained the same as a system of political domination and economic exploitation through indirect rule.
>
> The most glaring example of such hegemonic control was France. To hang on to their colonies, the French formed the French Community in 1958. That was the same year when France granted internal autonomy to all her colonies. It was also the same year in which Guinea demanded and won full independence and pulled out of the French Community. But the Community collapsed two years later in 1960 when all the French African colonies attained sovereign status. The French Community was formed to replace the imperialist French Union formed in 1946 and which was more brazen in its operations and pursuit of its imperial goals.[13]

This is interesting because of several reasons. To understand why the colonial masters took such actions, there are plenty of examples to provide us with insight. Apart from the general concepts such as unadulterated self-interest that are applicable here, there were geo-political developments that made the transition to neo-colonialism 'necessary'. If one navigates the official website of the EU, there is only one search result relating to the word 'colonialism' or the word 'colonies'. That search result is on the page 'History of the European Union 1960–69' and the reference to the colonies comes under the heading '20 July 1963' – the EEC signs its first big international agreement' and specifically states that:

> The 6 member countries sign the Yaoundé Convention to promote cooperation and trade with 18 former colonies in Africa. Today the EU has a special relationship of this kind with 79 countries in Africa, the Caribbean and Pacific (AFP) regions and is working to build a stronger partnership with Africa to tackle challenges common to both continents.[14]

We shall get to this 'special relationship' shortly, but what we have here is the founding members of the EEC – The European Economic Community – 'promoting cooperation and trade' with 18 former colonies, and those founding members were West Germany, France, Italy, Belgium, Luxembourg, and the Netherlands (the UK declined to join); or, in other words, countries that were central and pivotal in the destructive conquest of the African continent. The implication here is that the modern EU (that the EEC was folded into in the early 1990s) seems to be built upon the suffering of the African continent, without any official connection to the horrors that went before 'independence', but, as Hansen and Jonsson demonstrate, this moving away from responsibility cannot disguise the strategy of the early European cooperative models and the importance that colonialism had to the early post-War European model:

> Depending on the context, Eurafrica was asserted now as a necessity, now as a possibility, now as a common European task, now as a utopian future, now as a strategic interest, now as an economic imperative, now as a peace project, now as the white man's burden, now as Europe's last chance, now as Africa's only hope. Commentators, politicians and other moulders of public opinion who advocated the project tended to stress its epochal significance; Eurafrica was, quite simply, indispensable for Europe's geopolitical and economic survival. Of course, not everyone agreed with this view. There was strong opposition from many sides and, needless to say, the Africans scarcely has a say. 'At that time no one asked their opinion on the matter for they had no voice of their own' wrote Schofield Coryell in a 1962 issue of *Africa Today*.[15]

Not only was the African continent vital for the European community's economic development, but it had a more important role (at the cost, of course, to Africans and their home): providing for a shared mission that could unite the consistently divided continent. It was decided that the conflicts that were developing within the African continent because of the scramble for resources were proving to be a net-negative factor for all involved and that cooperation would further the shared cause. The African continent faced a united European continent rather than competing individuals. The push to make Africa 'Europe's plantation'[16] without continuing any sort of militaristic approach was well underway. A geo-political-sensitive approach was, therefore, adopted:

> Gradually, then, the economic perspective expanded into a geopolitical one, which touched the sensitive issue as to whether Europe would ever again attain its global influence. In this context we encounter the African continent, seen as a necessary condition for economic recovery and also as a sufficient reason for European unification. Coudenhove-Kalergi and Deutsch argued for European unity by way of a united colonial effort in Africa. In their view, Africa was seen as a natural and necessary part of Europe's geopolitical sphere, a part that needed to be more strongly

> connected to Europe, and to be exploited by united European forces in order to turn its resources to full advantage.[17]

Hansen and Jonsson's fascinating account concludes:

> [the coordinated approach to Africa was] beneficial that it constituted in itself a reason for European states to make common cause. A geopolitical calculation based on two symbiotic benefits emerged: the new geopolitical sphere of a united Europe would be sustainable and prosperous thanks to its incorporation of Africa; and correspondingly, the bonds between once-antagonistic European states would be consolidated by the shared goal of developing Africa. The unification of Europe and a unified European effort to colonize Africa were two processes that presupposed one another. Africa could be developed only by Europe, and Europe could develop its fullest potential only through Africa. As Coudenhove-Kalergi proclaimed: 'The African problem thus brings us back to Europe. Africa cannot be made available, if Europe does not unite.' In short, Europe's unification would start in Africa.[18]

In short, Europe's unification would start in Africa. This is a remarkable sentiment when we think of what happened next and that modern Europe chooses to forget about this history. The official history, according to the EU then, is that the new European entity simply entered into trading agreements with their former, now independent, colonies. There is a sense of equality in these statements that is not supported by facts because, in reality, there was nothing equal about these 'trading agreements'.

Omotola and Saliu describe an era of 'hopes and expectations' for African countries gaining their independence throughout the late 1950s and 1960s, on the basis that 'Africa's new leaders believed that, given the abundance of human and natural endowment at their disposal, they were bound to make steady progress in the direction of sustainable democratic governance and development'.[19] After gaining independence, the new states sought to 'change the rules of old international economic order and establish a "new international economic order" (NIEO) based on the principles of justice, sustainability, and equality between states'.[20] This planning for a new economic order was, as we know, being developed against a backdrop of concerted and strategic planning for the continuation of colonialism, though in a different format. The proposed new economic order did not, perhaps predictably, succeed. Scholars have suggested that it was not the idea of a new economic order that was the reason for its failure but the environment within which the idea was pitched, although I would argue this is one and the same thing. Mallard cites several scholars who argue that the neo-liberal revolution that gripped the UK and US in the 1980s with the Thatcher and Reagan administrations was to blame for defeating the ideas from the Global South, but we know that the developing EU was working to actively undermine the sovereignty of what were former colonies. In essence, what we have is a majoritively Global North shutdown of positive developments for former colonies.

The reality was that whilst new governments had hopes and expectations of economic development leading to political stability for the new entities, they stood no chance. In referencing the British experience with their colonies, Leigh Gardner presents a fascinating insight into the mindset of the colonisers when dealing with the practicalities of their colonies. Regarding the concepts of risk and investments, she cites John Maynard Keynes who complained in 1924 that

> perhaps the limit of the absurdity, to which the Trustee Acts can lead, was reached early this year when £2,000,000 was borrowed by Southern Rhodesia on about the same terms as a large English borough would have to pay . . . [Southern Rhodesia] is a place somewhere in the middle of Africa with a handful of white inhabitants and not even so many, I believe, as one million savage black ones.[21]

Despite Keynes' thoughts, there was a period when colonies could borrow on favourable terms, but that was only based on the presence of the 'empire-effect', which meant that the risk was reduced for investors because of the presence of a militaristic 'stick' (as opposed to a 'carrot') if non-payment became a possibility. Once that militaristic threat subsided as the colonisers began favouring non-militaristic approaches before eventually pulling back, officially, from the continent, the increased risk meant that many colonies and former colonies simply could not gain investment to develop their nations (inclusive of infrastructure needs that would have made post-colonial trade easier, such as the development of roads and rail across often differing terrains). Now, after being allowed to enter the global marketplace on their own two feet, nation states found that they were exposed to the harshness of the marketplace without the 'protection' of their colonial masters, and the effect was predictably impactful.[22]

Many of the new nations were heavily reliant on exporting their raw materials. Whilst a lack of investment during colonial times into the internal infrastructures effectively hamstrung the new nations, it was also the case that the economic environment at the time would not present favourable conditions for the new states. Relying heavily on natural resource exportation did not bode well when, in the mid-1970s, the price of oil nosedived after previously quadrupling. This led Mohammed Bedjaoui, the Algerian Ambassador who was sent to renegotiate the terms of a concessionary oil contract between Algeria and France, to write that 'debt service alone, namely annual amortization and interest payments, would exceed the total amount of new loans by 20 percent in Africa'.[23] Essentially, the vicious debt circle that we witness today had started in earnest for the new countries.

Omotola and Saliu make the interesting point that a few factors led to the new countries being in this predicament. In addition to being faced with a concerted neo-colonial response from their former conquerors and being exposed to the volatile global marketplace with no adequate protection, there was internal pressure. The promise of a better future away from the horrors of colonialism led to the new leaders being put under immense pressure from their own citizenry to deliver on the promises that had been made prior to independence.[24] This led to the new governments rushing to correct the impact of the wider marketplace and make deals, often in haste, that would ultimately cost their countries any sort of development potential. Mallard suggests that negotiators for the countries were too inexperienced or too quick to compromise when faced with their opponents from their former colonial masters.[25] Nevertheless, the result was a compromised start, laden with debt that they could not service, in a depressed economic environment that did not value the countries' main exports. As Gamarra et al. confirm, 'before the quadrupling of oil prices in 1973, requests for debt relief from developing countries were limited'.[26]

As a quick digression, the oil price issue needs to be explained. After a period of oil price control by the US, the breakout of the Yom Kippur war saw the Arab oil-producing states take action against Western militarisation. As Rauscher explains, 'in October 1973, the Yom Kippur war broke out. As a response to Western military support for Israel, the Arab oil-producing states decided to cut production by 5% and to impose an embargo on the USA and the Netherlands. Production was cut once again in November. This led to a reduction of Arab oil production by 5 million b/d or 24%. In December, the posted price for Arabian Light oil was raised by more than 400% to $11.65 per barrel'.[27] The effect of this external and volatile turmoil upon the new African states was instantaneous. Johnson and Wilson helpfully describe how 'the flood of high import prices that swept over African economies in the 1970s severely imbalanced their international payments accounts, knocked African development plans out of their traditional moorings, and nearly drowned the new states in a sea of debts'.[28] Interestingly, the scholars continue:

> African spokesmen, decrying what some called 'economic assassination', echoed voices raised in the industrial world charging OPEC with increasing the prices without cause or concern. Although African leaders and the media acknowledged that the causes for their increased import bills were indeed complex, they nevertheless believed that 'whether this plight is attributable to . . . increased . . . oil prices or other factors . . . is academic . . . Africa needs emergency assistance'. 'The oil weapon', they said, is 'intended for use against Israel's allies [but] instead [has] hurt those who supported the Arab cause'. The Africans thought the crisis was real only in its consequences, and not in its cases. That African economies have been injured is evident enough. Even in the stronger ones, the debris of unfinished development projects, devastated development plans, and the severe erosion of mass, if not elite hopes for a bright economic future give grim testimony that something important has happened. The proud, if

> somewhat meaningless and relatively modest, achievements of aggregate per capita growth rates of about 1.6 percent during the 1960s dropped to less than one percent during the 1970s, with the prospect of near stagnation for the 1980s, especially for non-oil-exporting African countries. Food production [had] fallen to critically low levels in a number of countries, and debt burdens [were] sacrificing such a large and rapidly growing share of exports, that some countries [were] fully exhausting their margin of investable surpluses.[29]

This exposure to the economic elements, as it were, without any real adequate protection from the colonisers who had granted the countries their 'freedom', resulted in the extraordinarily short-lived enjoyment of the freedom that came with independence. By the mid-1970s, large numbers of recently independent countries were in desperate need of help. That help, however, came at a price. Chaker argues, with conviction, that the post-colonial financial system was set up to take advantage of the issues that were inherent within the post-colonial states. The massive dollar-denominated debts 'did not arise from private exchange in a regulatory vacuum. Rather, they are the product of an international financial system carefully designed to facilitate neo-colonial extraction'.[30] Chaker qualifies this take with the view that 'debt is a vicious cycle that is neither free nor fair. A mix of dependency and deprivation has forced governments . . . to enter into debt in order to maintain basic living standards. A large share of income flows to the creditors at the top of the income distributions. In turn, the creditors invest their capital to lobby for law, regulations, and foreign policies in their favour'. Whilst Chaker is referring to general debt principles here, the point still stands. In the 1970s, which began the cycle of debt dependency for the new countries, the creditors were other countries and banks, and lobbying took the form of utilising multilateral institutions such as the World Bank and the IMF to implement debt giving but also debt controls. Chaker goes on to argue that

> the neo-colonial dynamics of debt are not only located in the narrow site of extraction, when the debtor actually coughs up cash to the creditor. Rather, they must be understood as a broad system that is designed to undermine popular sovereignty . . . [by using indebtedness] to shift power away from the people . . . and toward international financial institutions . . . that then dictate the rules and policies that govern everyday life.[31]

As we shall see, Chaker is correct because it has been noted that in relation to a mass debt crisis that erupted in 1982 (as just one example),

> the IMF and the World Bank practically oversaw the financial rescue policies that were necessary to address the mass debt crisis that erupted in 1982. Policies centred on 'structural adjustment' (mostly privatisation) and 'macroeconomic tightening' (austerity measures) were suggested and applied.[32]

We will look at 'structural adjustments' in the next section, but the impact is clear: the reduction in sovereignty and the reduced ability to thrive that comes with increased and predominantly internationalised privatisation, particularly when adjoined to strict and brutal austerity measures, is not hard to imagine. This is what led the president of Burkina Faso to state, in continuation of an earlier quote in the book: 'Debt is colonialism . . . debt is a skilfully managed reconquest of Africa, intended to subjugate its growth and development through foreign rules'.[33] Let us remember this as we now work our way through analysing some of the key instances of multilateral debt treatment that mainly affected/affects the African continent.

1.4 Multilateral Debt Treatment Under Review

On the back of the tumultuous start for the new sovereign states, what followed would be crisis after crisis, with the international community subsequently developing particular programmes to provide 'assistance' to the affected states. However, as we are attempting to view the genealogical development of debt treatment through a critical lens, Roodman's suggestion that a 'crisis' is not a crisis at all if it is continuous, but more of a 'chronic syndrome'[34] provides us with a good place to start this section.

However, before we do that, there is an interesting digression to make that will enable us to more accurately understand what followed for the states in question. That digression takes the form of a question: 'what is the reason for the failures?' Clearly, for so many states to be suffering financially, something must be 'wrong'. Fole suggests that there are three contending explanations that have been given and held sway. The first is that all of the financial difficulties that vulnerable states find themselves in are because of governmental policy failure. This view believes that well-researched and 'orthodox macroeconomic management' is the best way for a country to economically recover and thus what is needed is for experts to apply 'structural adjustment' to organisationally create a better system to economically recover. This view is held by the World Bank and the IMF and has its roots in the 'Berg Report' from the beginning of the 1980s. The next view that Fole cites argues that the problems for the vulnerable countries emanate from deficiencies regarding basic economic and social infrastructure, research capability, technological know-how, and human resource development, which are all compounded by problems of socio-political organisation.[35] This leads to the pronouncements that structural adjustment is not only the wrong diagnosis but also the wrong treatment. This view was developed by the Economic Commission for Africa (ECA) in their 1989 report entitled 'African Alternative Framework for Structural Adjustment Programmes for Socio-Economic Recovery and Transformation'. Furthermore, Fole argues that the reason for the plight of the vulnerable countries in question emanates from a deep economic dependence. This view suggests that 'the problems are best understood as resulting from long-term underdevelopment'.[36] This view is what Fole calls the 'Marxist view', held and developed by prominent Marxist scholars.

What is clear to see here is that the host perhaps determines the argument of who or what is to blame for the consistent predicament that vulnerable countries find themselves in. The 'structural adjustment' policies will be something we will look at in detail very shortly, but in short, it is the imposition of austerity measures and new governance policies from those who can provide help. The approach is steeped in economic theory and has been applied very liberally by multilateral institutions since the late 1970s and 1980s. This is despite the widespread understanding that 'structural adjustment' does not work (as evidenced by the continuation of debt troubles and dependency) and is often to blame for the continuation of those troubles, as Roodman suggests:

> Structural adjustment lending faced another layer of problems. Not only was the structural adjustment advice of questionable value, it often went unheeded – or was unneeded. In dozens of case studies, independent economists and political scientists have documented how borrowing governments typically sidestepped the promises they made in adjustment agreements with the World Bank and the IMF, obeyed the letter but not the spirit, or agreed to steps they would have taken anyway.[37]

The ECA and prominent Marxists have acknowledged and highlighted that the historical underdevelopment of the vulnerable countries makes sense, given their constitution: direct knowledge and experience of the transition from colonialism to neo-colonialism is bound to make such historical connections very clear. However, for the World Bank and IMF to essentially blame the victim makes sense too because for the Western-led institutions to recognise and factor in the appalling effects of colonialism on the new states means accepting responsibility. The impacts of colonialism are clear, and so is the responsibility to help former colonies develop (even before independence, in truth). As we now navigate our way through the developments that led to formal debt treatment initiatives, let us not ignore this 'elephant in the room' as so many have, and continue to choose to do, as it is an inescapable truth that must be factored in.

Returning to our linear story, it is true that before the oil crisis in the early 1970s, very few countries requested help with their debt.[38] From the time that the World Bank was launched in 1946 up until 1972 just before the onset of the oil crisis, only nine countries had sought help. As the predominant constitution of a sovereign state's creditors were other countries and official creditors, such as the multilateral institutions, or a handful of banking organisations, a framework was quickly set up to forge agreements on how to provide assistance. Under the auspices of the 'Paris Club' – made up of creditor nations – and the 'London Club' – made up of influential creditor banks, it was agreed very early on that:

> low-income countries were confronting short-term liquidity crises and that rescheduling of debt service would provide sufficient breathing space

> and debt relief to enable them to get back on an even keel and grow out of their debt problems.[39]

We shall see in this and the next few chapters that this approach, developed almost half a century ago, is still the favoured approach for the financial system. Many African countrieswere being drowned by their debt because they had borrowed against the commodities that they had, although the oil price issue coincided with a similar impact on the price and volatility of commodities. The boom in the price of commodities that had gone before did not last, and the collapse in commodity prices in the mid-1970s, coupled with the volatility in the price of oil, left many new countries at the mercy of the market, and we already know that it did not end well.

If we leave the argument that debt dependency and the continuation of debt issues are truly engrained and almost philosophical concerns relating to right and wrong for a moment and focus only on the economic elements of debt and credit, then some aspects must be acknowledged. For example, if a creditor, or set of creditors, has a different understanding of the capabilities of the debtor than the reality of the debtor's situation describes, then short-term debt treatment is unlikely to be impactful. This has been suggested to be the case in the 1970s and 1980s when official and private creditors were faced with an 'avalanche' of debt treatment requests from the world's most vulnerable. Gamarra et al. describe how, for the creditors, the simple aim was to 'determine the minimum amount of relief to be granted to allow debtors to pay their remaining debt service without recourse to further debt relief'.[40] Very clinical and very economically minded. However, such theoretical approaches rarely take anything else into account, such as the history between the creditor and the debtor or the socio-political foundations within the debtor. This proved to be costly because although creditors insisted on debtors only receiving short-term assistance at market rates, that is, no concessions were made, and debtors were forced to take the blame and embark upon internal changes akin to structural adjustment, the end result was a simple one:

> By the end of 1986, the Paris Club had restructured the debt of 22 Sub-Saharan African countries in 55 agreements. Between 1973 and 1986, 14 African countries went to the Paris Club more than once, and 9 went three times or more. The principle that debts once rescheduled were not to be rescheduled proved unworkable. In almost half of the 55 agreements signed with African countries during this period, creditors were forced to restructure previously rescheduled claims.[41]

Having to restructure already-restructured debt points at the failure of creditors to provide ample assistance to nudge a challenged debtor towards the financial health needed to repay the original debt. It is the direct result of a short-term mindset that underestimates the plight of the debtor. To try to learn from these lessons, the IMF and World Bank developed the novel 'Special Program of

Assistance' (SPA) for low-income and debt-distressed countries in sub-Saharan Africa in the fall of 1987. This was, essentially, the first example of a coordinated and international approach to dealing with debt treatment on the African continent. The aim was to promote economic growth in eligible countries; to be counted as eligible, there were three stages to consider. The first was that countries had to be defined as 'low-income'; this was determined by being eligible for concessional loans from the World Bank's International Development Association (IDA). The second stage to eligibility was that the country had to be defined as being 'debt distressed', which was qualified as having a debt-service-to-export ratio of 30% or more. The final stage for being eligible for the SPA was that the country had to be 'engaged in adjustment', meaning that the country had to be seen to agree and start implementing adjustment programmes designed by the IMF and IDA.[42]

The lack of impact from the Paris Club and the creation of the first internationally coordinated assistance programme began a wave of initiatives and pushes to provide assistance. Just before the SPA had been set up, the G-7 Summit meeting in Venice communicated that any African countries participating in structural adjustment efforts 'should be given to the possibility of applying lower interest rates on their existing debt and agreement should be reached, especially in the Paris Club, on longer repayment and grace periods to ease the debt burden'. This saw Mauritania, Mozambique, Somalia, and Uganda declared eligible for this special treatment and their repayment terms on outstanding non-concessional debt increased to 20 years, with a 10-year grace period.[43] The year after, G-7 leaders went further and communicated, from the Toronto Summit, that IDA-eligible countries could have their non-concessional, official bilateral, and guaranteed commercial debt reduced by up to 33% in net present value terms. All creditors were subsequently given a menu of options to achieve this aim, which consisted of options such as outright cancellation or reducing interest rates to below-market rates.

What followed, before we get to the first of the four initiatives that this chapter will pay particular attention to, were the 'Trinidad terms' and the 'Naples terms'. The Trinidad terms, proposed by the UK in 1990, presented ideas to reduce the net present value of future debt service repayments, and this was then actioned in the cases of the Arab Republic of Egypt and Poland the following year. The Naples terms then attempted to build on this around 1995 and sought to provide for an ultimate 'exit' from the rescheduling process, via concerted adjustments. Whilst ambitious, and in keeping with the economic doctrines that had come before, the reality was an abject failure. Of all 37 countries that had concluded agreements in Naples terms between 1995 and 2008, only two (Cambodia and Yemen) eventually exited the process because their debt profile had been reduced to a sustainable level; all the other countries soon migrated to the 'Heavily Indebted Poor Countries' (HIPC) initiative, which is where our four-stage analysis starts.

However, before we do that, there is something worth acknowledging. This continuous development of debt treatment initiatives, leading to failure after failure on behalf of the international community because, lest we forget, every failure leads to the continuation of poverty and deprivation for the citizens of each country involved, is a stain on the international community. I shall not return to Fola's excellent account of the reasons for failure, but there is indeed a clear disconnect between the willingness of the creditors and the capabilities of the debtors. Roodman tells us that 'one thing that did not change was the implicit assumption that experts in Washington, D.C., could analyse societies far different from their own well enough to give governments reliable and realistic advice'.[44] This makes sense, of course, but has never changed. The lack of flexibility and refusal to engage in collaborative and cooperative measures on behalf of the international community is yet another stain. This theme will be repeated as we continue through the major international efforts to bring debt crises under control on the African continent (and beyond).

1.5 The Heavily Indebted Poor Countries (HIPC) Initiative 1996

The mid-1990s saw the next formal debt treatment initiative put together. It has been said that the concept of the HIPC initiative was to 'wipe off the debt and allow countries to get their affairs in order',[45] but this is exceptionally simplistic. The HIPC initiative began a theoretically new phase of debt treatment for vulnerable countries in that write-downs were more of a viable option, but the fact that the initiative was supplemented by a new initiative only a decade later – the Multilateral Debt Relief Initiative (MDRI) – tells us that the HIPC initiative still had room to be much better than it was. However, it was impactful.

The criteria for eligibility were very similar to the eligibility criteria for the SPA. There were two 'points' in the initiative: a decision point and a completion point. First, a country had to fulfil four particular conditions:

1. Be eligible to borrow from the World Bank's International Development Agency, which provides interest-free loans and grants to the world's poorest countries, and from the IMF's Poverty Reduction and Growth Trust, which provides loans to low-income countries at subsidised rates
2. Must have faced an unsustainable debt burden that cannot be addressed through traditional debt relief mechanisms
3. Must have established a track record of reform and sound policies through IMF- and World Bank-supported programmes
4. Must have developed a Poverty Reduction Strategy Paper (PRSP) through a board-based participatory process in the country

The executive boards of the two multilateral institutions then decided, based on the progress the country makes, whether the country can begin receiving relief. However, this relief was only on an interim basis. To reach the 'completion point' and take full advantage of the initiative by receiving full and irrevocable relief, a country must

1 Establish a further track record of good performance under programmes supported by loans from the IMF and the World Bank
2 Implement satisfactorily key reforms agreed at the decision point
3 Adopt and implement its PRSP for at least one year[46]

The initial rate of countries reaching the completion point was a remarkably high 92%. However, we must note here that for a country to go from phase one to phase two, there was a three-year period in which the country must show compliance with the criteria of the post-decision point phase.[47] After reaching the decision point, countries would be eligible to be considered under the Naples terms agreement, with a two-thirds debt stock reduction possible. There were another three years of compliance to be witnessed if a country was to make it past the 'completion point'. The reward for this was the potential of an 80% reduction in all debt stock.

The IMF stated that the aims of the initiative were not just related to debt relief but to ensure that savings made from the initiative were funnelled to those that were in desperate need of support. One example that the IMF highlight is that before the HIPC initiative was started, countries were spending more on debt servicing than they were on health and education throughout their jurisdictions. The IMF report that in the aftermath of the HIPC initiative, countries were spending up to five times more on their social infrastructures than on serving their debts. They were also keen to note that the way in which poorer countries managed their public debt had gotten significantly better as a result of the initiative. In arguing for the benefits of structural adjustment, the IMF noted that 'debt relief has markedly improved the debt position of post-completion point countries, bringing their debt indicators down below those of other HIPCs or non-HIPCs'.[48]

The HIPC initiative represented a 'turning point', according to scholars and onlookers.[49] However, we need to be careful with this because there is more than one perspective to consider here. On one hand, things were very different with this initiative. On the other hand, some aspects were frustratingly similar. For example, whilst the IMF chose to maintain the blind ambition that the initiative represented the 'exit' from debt troubles for the affected countries – a view that does not consider historical or non-economic understandings of the situation – the presence of civil society for the first time was considered to be a welcome development. 'Civil society' is a catch-all term for organisations such as non-profit organisations, non-governmental organisations, charities, philanthropic endeavours, and grassroots organisations. Unhelpfully, as Edwards comments, 'civil society is one of the most enduring and confusing concepts in social science',[50] although the World Economic Forum defined it as a 'diverse and ever-wide ecosystem of individuals, communities, and organisations'.[51] The ever-changing nature of the civil society world makes a clear and concise definition almost impossible, but the point here is that the introduction of resourced and organised external bodies that could research, organise, and campaign on behalf of the vulnerable was a 'game changer'. Today, numerous influential civil society groups have transformed their offerings to just being concerned with the plight of the world's most vulnerable countries, and the HIPC initiative was perhaps the first instance of coordinated pressure against the financial elite on a global level.

Whilst I referenced an IMF report earlier that stated that a high percentage of those eligible for the HIPC initiative went through to the completion point, the report I utilised is from recent times and is written in hindsight. When looked at in terms of the development of the initiative as it went through, things were not always so rosy. As we know, one of the main requirements from the IMF at the outset of the initiative was that countries had to be able to demonstrate a track record of policy and reform implementation. However, it has been confirmed that the IMF had to reduce the importance of this criterion in the 'enhanced HIPC' initiative, which was established in 1999,[52] because the countries could not 'demonstrate an ability to put such frameworks in place, which raises concerns about the achievement of the HIPC objectives'.[53]

There were other problems with the HIPC initiative. Lala et al. rightly note that in addition to important elements of financial sustainability such as export diversification being outside of the mandate for the HIPC initiative, 'debtors cannot oblige creditors to participate in debt relief under voluntary initiatives. Involving both creditors and debtors at the design stage of the proposals for debt relief can be an important step in disseminating information about the workings of the initiative and securing the cooperation of all creditors'.[54] This is a vital element to understand because the HIPC initiative, along with every other debt treatment initiative we shall review, is voluntary. This has the effect of allowing two particular groups to erect hurdles in the race to aid with debt unsustainability within the vulnerable countries. For example, in the HIPC initiative, the IMF confirm:

> Another challenge is to ensure that eligible countries get full debt relief from all their creditors. Although the largest creditors (the World Bank, the African Development Bank, the IMF, the Inter-American Development Bank, and all Paris Club creditors) have provided their full share of debt relief under the HIPC Initiative, and even beyond, others are lagging behind. Smaller plurilateral institutions, non-Paris Club official bilateral creditors, and commercial creditors, which together account for about 26 percent of total HIPC Initiative costs, have so far only delivered a small share of their expected relief. Non – Paris Club bilateral creditors as a whole have delivered around 51 percent of their share of HIPC Initiative debt relief, but about one third of these creditors have not delivered any relief at all. While there has been some increase in the delivery over the past few years, the rate of delivery remains disappointingly low. The delivery of debt relief by commercial creditors has increased markedly in recent

> years through a few large operations supported by IDA's Debt Reduction Facility buyback operations. Some commercial creditors have initiated litigations against HIPCs, raising significant legal challenges to burden sharing among all creditors, including the multilateral institutions. The number of litigation cases against HIPCs has been declining in recent years and flattened over the past few years.[55]

Towards the end of this chapter and in future chapters, we shall see that the role of private creditors and non-Paris Club creditors relatively exploded in the new millennium, and particularly after the Financial Crisis. This voluntary nature of the debt treatment initiatives is, therefore, a liability that is often very costly for vulnerable countries. This is because of the political power plays that exist on the global level, and the IMF and World Bank can only do so much in reality – as they suggest when the IMF says that they will 'continue to use moral suasion to encourage creditors to participate'.[56] We can, therefore, see that one of the HIPC initiative's 'guiding principles', that is, 'the provision of debt relief should be coordinated by all creditors, with broad and equitable participation'[57] was simply not achieved.

Nevertheless, the HIPC initiative had started the world along a very different path in terms of coordinated multilateral debt treatment initiatives. The money essentially saved by vulnerable countries by participating in the HIPC initiative varies from just under and just above $100 billion, but the importance of changing tack towards debt reduction was a very important one. Whilst key lessons were not learned, the HIPC initiative represented an early attempt to provide true financial support rather than just some financial breathing space. Lessons would need to be learned, and we shall now see in the next few sections whether that was indeed the case. Lessons such as not being lured into the attractive notion that one initiative can bring the continent up to par with the western world are perhaps the most important because if the 'powers that be' continue to have this 'exit' strategy as their core strategy, the proof is visible for all to see that it simply will not work. Aiming for an end-all 'cure' without considering the historical and non-economic understandings of the African situation is a fool's errand, and we shall now see whether that continued.

1.6 The Jubilee 2000 Attempt

The arrival of civil society on the scene immediately began to have an effect. Historically, decisions have been made about the future of the African continent (and many others outside of the continent) without their input or even a voice to put forward their perspective, but the force of civil society changed that. This is not to say that civil society was or is perfect because it is often very fractured and there can be duplication or competition of interest that fragments the force witnessed. Nevertheless, there can be an absence of political agenda that allows members and organisations within civil society to work collaboratively with those affected so that their voice and experiences can be directly injected into the decision-making process, for better or worse. Whilst the HIPC initiative had started a development pathway for vulnerable countries, there were still political agendas at play alongside the preservation of the creditor rather than the advancement of the position of the debtor. The 'Jubilee Campaign' in 2000 sought to change that.

The campaign effectively started in 1990. The Politics academic, Martin Dent, wrote extensively from his position at Keele University – having spent time in the British Indian Army and then as a Colonial Civil Servant in Nigeria – about the biblical concept of 'jubilee' and how it could be translated for the modern world.[58] Although the idea was met mostly with scepticism, towards the end of the decade, Dent and Bill Peters approached the Debt Crisis Network (DCN), which consisted of the largest British aid agencies coordinating research and work on debt treatment in the third world. Nevertheless, his ideas were widely rejected as being too religious in connotation.[59] It was suggested eventually within the DCN that the concept could resonate with large and influential faith-based organisations, as well as with people around the world as it moved towards the year 2000. The concept of Jubilee, as Dent put it forward, was that it constituted a biblical mandate to periodically cancel debts, free slaves, and restore land to its vital owners, and the campaign began to focus on the cancellation of debts as being potentially the most impactful element of the whole campaign. The idea began to gain momentum, and as one of the campaign's key people Ann Pettifor stated, 'the effect was electrifying'.[60] Formerly, the campaign launched in 1997 and used a chain as its symbol, which had the aim of

> referring to international campaigning against the slave trade in the nineteenth century, representing the enslaving nature of the debt burden – and conversely, coming more positively to represent the human links, the chain of activists linking hands in solidarity.[61]

The campaign's aim of appealing to people and organisations of faith proved to be a shrewd one. The first supporters of the campaign were 'evangelical Christians organised around the aid agency TearFund'. Pettifor tells us that 'the Debt Crisis Network's approach to debt cancellation was radical by their standards, as indeed was the political analysis of the injustice of global finance'.[62] From there, the campaign grew to develop coalitions and partner campaigns in nearly 70 countries and contained more than 100 member organisations at the turn of the millennium.

In terms of judging whether the campaign was successful, it all depends on one's perspective. The World Bank confirmed that the initiative eventually led to the cancellation of more than $100 billion worth of debt for the most vulnerable nations, which is astounding for an initiative that was alive for just over three years.[63] Birdsall et al. argue differently, agreeing that it was a success because 'it succeeded not just in changing official policy but in arousing a measure of concern among the world's rich about the state of the world's poor that had been conspicuously lacking for many years'.[64] Busby suggests that the campaign was a political success in that it forced creditor governments to accept deeper debt reduction at the G8 Cologne Summit in 1999.[65] However, the reality that the debt reduction came via the Cologne Summit means that there must have been more pressure than just from the Jubilee Campaign, and others, such as Yanacopulos, have been eager to point this out:

> This was a result of the sustained efforts of a number of essential players including Non-Governmental Organizations (NGOs), civil society groups, governments, and the International Financial Institutions (IFIs), resulting in the G7 governments competing over who could write-off the most debt during the 1999 Cologne summit. Without the sustained efforts of certain groups within the 'debt network' such as Oxfam International and Jubilee 2000, this cancellation would not have occurred.[66]

Thus, it is abundantly clear that the Jubilee 2000 campaign was very successful in providing a compelling narrative to generate public pressure. However, it is important to remember that the pressure came from many parts of the civil society sector. Some go further, with Buxton writing that 'yet three years after the campaign's set deadline of 2000 for radical debt relief, the international anti-debt movement has lost much of its momentum and the promises made by creditor governments and institutions appear increasingly hollow'.[67] As we will look at the MDRI in Section 1.8, perhaps his understanding is astute in that the lasting impact of the Jubilee Campaign and the others from across civil society was limited at best. However, this is a very limited view on the concept of 'impact'. To finish the section, I found that Mayo's take on the impact of the campaign provides us with an illustration of a larger and much more lasting impact that was achieved:

> The campaign challenged predominant constructions of indebtedness and questioned neoliberal development strategies more generally. In addition, Jubilee 2000 challenged negative images of the poor in the South as passive 'victims' of capitalist globalisation. The most prevalent images of developing countries, it has been argued, remain Live Aid-type images of starving children with flies around their eyes, too weak to brush them off, dependent upon the resources and knowledge of the industrialised countries in the North to progress. In contrast, Jubilee 2000 provided an example of a mobilisation to promote change through solidarity rather than through charity, however well-meaning.[68]

This correction of a long-held narrative was radical at the time and has proven to be crucial.

1.7 The Idea of the Sovereign Debt Restructuring Mechanism

Though the environment regarding the thinking of debt treatment solutions had fundamentally changed with the injection of the voices emanating from civil society endeavours, there was an associated effect that would lead the world towards considering a new solution. The slow-but-steady move to an environment within which debt reductions, and sometimes particularly heavy reductions, were becoming prevalent began to attract the attention of Western minds. Rather than waiting until a country could not meet their financial obligations and then holding debt treatment discussions from a position of crisis, the idea that a formal bankruptcy procedure could be set up to facilitate debt discussions between debtor and creditor, with the aim of the country returning to some sort of position where they could meet their obligations, was being crystallised.

This section is concerned with the proposed 'Sovereign Debt Restructuring Mechanism' that was proposed by the IMF in 2002, but there is a body of literature that come well before that date that formed the technical and ideological basis for the SDRM idea. One of the first ideas came from Christopher Oechsli in 1981, who put forward the argument that something akin to Chapter 11 (of the US Bankruptcy Reform Act) bankruptcy proceedings in the US should be established for sovereign debtors.[69] Oechsli is widely credited as starting the idea for a formal structure, but in reality, ideas had been put forward even before this point, with a group of 77 developing countries in 1979 proposing something called the 'International Debt Commission' at their meeting in Arusha. Predictably, their proposal never came to fruition because of resistance from debtor countries, but the main aim of the proposal was to make creditor–debtor relations more favourable to debtors, or at least more favourable than the terms found within the Paris Club; there was not any real focus on the interplay between creditors as such.[70] Nevertheless, Oechsli does detail a broad and formal procedure for the restructuring of sovereign debt and, as Rogoff and Zettelmeyer discuss, his idea had many important facets to it. First, in terms of the translatability of the Chapter 11 proceedings, Oechsli argues that three particular processes – a creditor committee, an independent examiner, and a formal initiation procedure – would coalesce to provide for a much fairer and more reliable debt restructuring procedure, which is sorely needed because:

> According to Oechsli, sovereign debt restructuring under the status quo suffers from several problems. Negotiations take too long, and their outcome is too uncertain, harming the debtor and delaying the rehabilitation process. Moreover, they may be insufficiently focused on 'LDC's basic development as the means to strengthen the country's credit and debt service capacity'. In Oecshli's view, this is due to the 'lack of an established procedure' and poor creditor coordination.[71]

Interestingly, Oechsli suggests that whilst a court-like system could be put in place, with the IMF being capable of holding court, this is not necessary. Rather, the idea is that creditors (and debtors) could agree before contracting for the debt a particular arbitration procedure that suits both parties. The focus on arbitration is interesting because of its prevalence in modern commercial law, which is derived from its many advantages for parties, including speed, cost, and the lack of adversarial nature. These elements were, are, and will continue to be much needed in the field of sovereign debt.

Perhaps representing the time it was written, Oechsli concluded that the inefficacies in the sovereign debt field come from the official creditors and not the private creditors. As he was writing in the early 1980s, this makes sense. The majority of sovereign debt was held by official creditors, and the private creditor landscape was much smaller and less effectual than what we see today, consisting mainly of large banking institutions. He chose to underplay the collective action problems that emanated from the private sector, but the question is then raised whether arbitration is strong enough to house and control creditor countries and their agendas.

This idea of a Chapter 11-like process was built upon eventually. Before the concept of a more formal process was developed by Cohen in the late 1980s,[72] Sachs had challenged the concept of 'collective action' and discussed its applicability to the sovereign debt arena. Collective action problems essentially detail when there are barriers to bringing the majority to consensus; however, it is even more acute when *everybody* has to be in agreement to alter elements of a contract, for example. The following year in 1985, the ruling in the 'Allied Bank International v. Banco Credito Agricola de Cartago' case had the effect of making it crystal clear that Chapter 11 did not apply to sovereign debt restructurings. This also had the effect of allowing for 'holdout creditors' to continue as a practice, which is when if even just one creditor refuses to participate, the restructuring as agreed cannot go ahead. This ability to 'holdout' is an issue that remains with us today because it is grounded in the understanding that a creditor, having signed the agreement with the debtor, will always be able to expect to be paid in full.

Cohen's idea, in building on Oechsli's idea of a bankruptcy structure goes further in formalising the concept in the statute. He presents the idea of an 'International Debt Restructuring Agency' (IDRA), which would be a joint subsidiary of the IMF and World Bank and whose job, essentially, would be to become an administrative facilitator, mediator, and monitor for all sovereign debt transactions. As part of the process, Cohen envisages a creditor committee to come together when dealing with potential restructurings that would need less than unanimous agreement to go forward with the restructurings. This would, in effect, kill the collective action and 'free riding' problems.

As the Jubilee movement passed, it was and remains the case that an international Chapter 11-like process had not been set up. The IMF had two particular reasons to change this. The first was the identified 'moral hazards' in providing 'bailouts' to debtor countries because those debtor countries

> had little incentive . . . to engage in restructuring negotiations because the IMF often provided 'bailout loans'. The IMF has made it clear, however, that it no longer intends to provide these bailouts forcing the illiquid

> sovereign to choose between defaulting on its outstanding debt and ruining its creditworthiness, or participating in the restructuring process.[73]

Whilst it is important to challenge this perception that the IMF was simply handing out bailout loans and that this process was somehow easier or more beneficial than renegotiating with one's creditors, the IMF were central in the sovereign debt arena and thus had numerous reasons to seek to establish something more formal. One element was that their founding Articles did not permit them to bind creditors; thus, the need for a formal process to potentially do so was of real interest within the IMF. There was also a return to focusing on the issue of sovereign debt treatment as the Asian Financial Crisis began to subside in the early 2000s which had diverted people's attention from the sovereign issue[74] as many countries around the world began running into financial difficulties. The time was now, as far as the IMF was concerned, to play their hand.

In the 2002 Report entitled 'A New Approach to Sovereign Debt Restructuring', the IMF's new First Deputy Managing Director Anne Krueger laid out the vision for the IMF's formal 'Sovereign Debt Restructuring Mechanism'.[75] The proposal had foundations from within the literature and built upon ideas whereby the IMF would play a very important role, yet it would not be a central role; the aim was to induce collaborative and collective sentiment from the creditors and give them a structure within which they could work better together rather than a central institution (the IMF) taking the lead and compelling actors to find solutions because, as mentioned previously, the IMF does not have a mandate for that type of action. Krueger, in explaining the objectives of the SDRM, said:

> The objective of an SDRM is to facilitate the orderly, predictable, and rapid restructuring of unsustainable sovereign debt, while protecting asset values and creditors' rights. If appropriately designed and implemented, such a mechanism could help to reduce the costs of a restructuring for sovereign debtors and their creditors, and contribute to the efficiency of international capital markets more generally.[76]

Krueger helpfully details how the mechanism would work, with the IMF and World Bank also providing explainers. The process could only be initiated at the request of the debtor, with the aim being to protect the vulnerable debtor and allow it to be in control of the trigger point at which the mechanism would kick in. The SDRM is imagined to only need to be used in a very limited set of circumstances, according to Krueger, and would only apply to *insolvent* debtors rather than *illiquid* ones. The threshold for initiating the mechanism would be when the debt is deemed 'unsustainable' but before there is a clear need for any sort of debt reduction. Euliss explains that for debt to be deemed unsustainable, a country's debt-to-GDP ratio has to rise 'incessantly'. He suggests that a country may raise its taxes to be able to afford to service its debt portfolio, but this will inevitably stop economic growth and, as such, there can be no long-term debt sustainability. This, coupled with the requirement to reduce their hard currency reserves for paying off the debt and servicing loans in foreign denominations, results in a picture of unsustainability that would, theoretically, trigger the mechanism.[77]

In simple terms, the mechanism was designed to bring creditors together and provide a framework that could change the legal nature of creditors contracting with debtors. As the World Bank spell out,

> the SDRM would provide a legal mechanism for binding a minority of creditors to a debt restructuring agreed upon between a supermajority of creditors and the debtor. New finance would be shielded from restructuring. At the same time, creditor interests would be protected, including the prohibition of payments to nonpriority creditors and sanctions against abuse of the mechanism.[78]

In addition, the World Bank confirm that for this all to take place, there would need to be a force of law behind the planned aspects of the mechanism, and to achieve this, the IMF would need 'an amendment to the IMF's Articles of Agreement, which requires agreement by three-fifths of the IMF's members holding 85 percent of voting power, and which would be binding on all members'. This is important because as we shall see, the constitution of the IMF would play a key role in deciding whether the SDRM would be implemented.

There are many prospective positives to the SDRM being implemented. The first and most obvious positive is that it would eliminate the opportunity and rationale behind being a 'holdout' creditor, which would fundamentally hasten the restructuring process. In addition, whilst the mechanism would not be costless for the insolvent debtor, it would be much cheaper than either defaulting or undertaking costly measures in attempting to avoid the inevitable default. It would also reduce the burden on the multilateral institutions to provide financial support for the insolvent because the restructuring, as long as it was successful (the chances of which would be increased because of the structure of the SDRM), would provide the necessary support for the debtor in question in advance of an irretrievable crisis. The mechanism would also provide certainty going forward for all parties as the intricacies of the mechanism would be injected into the pricing of the debt in the first place.[79] Lastly, for reasons that will become clearer as we traverse through the book, it would be credit-positive that credit rating agencies could consider when producing a sovereign rating; the reduction in risk for the creditor in terms of non-payment and a reduction in potential legal costs could, in theory, make the vulnerable regions that much more investable.

However, where there are potential advantages, there are bound to be potential disadvantages; in the case of the SDRM, there are several. One of the largest questions that hung over the SDRM was whether it was even needed. The World Bank put forward an argument that shows, historically, there is no great need for the restructurings of the insolvent; they have been few and far between, and when they have happened, there have been very few products involved (in terms of loan products) and the creditors have been relatively easy to bring together. The World Bank continues by identifying a common worry within bankruptcy proceedings and the potential for 'strategic defaults'. The World Bank continues: 'if a solvent debtor can choose to default and use the SDRM as a shield against legal redress, then creditors would be less willing to provide funds in the first place'. However, this fear is easily countered. The SDRM has a particular threshold that must be evidenced before crossing and would have had the ability to issue sanctions for the misuse of the mechanism. In addition,

> creditors could refuse to support a restructuring proposal (or a proposal relating to priority financing) by a debtor they considered solvent. Moreover, the current proposal would enable creditors to terminate the use of the SDRM. Thus, the ability of solvent debtors to use the SDRM as a shield against making debt-service payments is limited.[80]

Another issue within any sort of debt treatment relates to the relationship *between* creditors. Usually, and especially within sovereign bond dealings, a creditor may not know exactly to who else the country owes money. This can breed distrust or an individualistic agenda that can be exceptionally damaging to a restructuring. For instance:

> The SDRM could increase investor uncertainty regarding the outcome and fairness of negotiations. An investor might be willing to agree to a collective action clause that facilitates restructuring of an individual bond by majority of the bondholders, but be reluctant to commit to a restructuring dictated by a majority of all creditors. The investor might lack knowledge about the compositions and interests of all creditors and the terms on other instruments, and be more uncertain about the outcome of a debt negotiation involving all creditors. An investor might be concerned that larger creditors could impose a restructuring that serves their longer-term interests (for example, maintaining relationships with the debtor) rather than gains the maximum from current negotiations.
>
> . . . this potential underlines the importance of increasing the information on the universe of a country's creditors in the context of bond offerings'.[81]

This relates to another key issue in the arena of sovereign debt treatment: the changed nature of the creditor base. The previous model for debt financing for a sovereign was rooted in official and private debt. Private debt was majoritively made up of large banking institutions, that is, easy to bring together, and often open to bilateral and multilateral suasion (for example, if a particular banking institution was synonymous with the country where it was based). However, at the turn of the millennium but even more so today, this landscape changed dramatically. Now, the credit markets have overtaken the banking institutions, and whilst the 'Universal Owners' have stakes in the developing world (a 'Universal Owner' is a large-scale institutional investor that is so large that it would have investments in the majority of markets), they are certainly not alone. This diverse and diffuse nature of creditors can cause serious problems for debt treatment initiatives, as Krueger explains:

> The move away from commercial bank lending as a source of external finance for emerging market sovereigns has made the coordination of creditors much more difficult than it was in the 1980s. Many creditors have no ongoing business relationship with the debtor to protect and are not subject to suasion by the official sector. The number and diversity of creditors has increased, with an associated increase in the diversity of interests and appetite for risk. These changes have been accompanied by an increase in the complexity of creditor claims. These developments have made creditor organization more complicated. A sovereign restructuring may require coordination across many bond issues, as well as syndicated loans and trade financing. This organization problem has been exacerbated by the repackaging of creditor claims in ways that separate the interests between the primary lender (the lender of record) and the end investor (the beneficiaries that hold the economic interest).
>
> Sovereigns with unsustainable debt burdens and a diffuse group of creditors can face substantial difficulties getting creditors collectively to agree to a restructuring agreement that brings the sovereign's debt down to a sustainable level. In particular, it may be difficult to secure high participation by creditors in a debt restructuring that would be in the interest of creditors as a group, as individual creditors may consider that their best interests would be served by trying to free ride in the hope of ultimately receiving payments in line with their original contracts. Both fears of free riding and other issues of intercreditor equity may inhibit creditors from accepting a proposed debt restructuring, prolonging the restructuring process and making it less likely that a deal will achieve the objective of restoring sustainability.[82]

Another problem with the concept of an IMF-initiated mechanism is that there are other options, legally, that would do the job and need much less reform to come to fruition. We shall cover this concept in detail when looking at the DSSI in the modern day, but the concept of a 'Collective Action Clause' (CAC) is of key interest here. A CAC is simply an aspect inserted into a bond contract that allows for a qualified majority of creditors in that bond to legally agree, before a crisis hits, to a specified and legally binding debt restructuring process. This fundamentally stops 'holdout' creditors because signing up to the bond that includes a CAC means every creditor is bound by the CAC. As the majority of developing world sovereign bonds are placed within the New York or English jurisdictions, as well as in the EU, the availability of the option of

CACs in those jurisdictions potentially limits the need for the SDRM. Krueger acknowledges this and suggests that 'the inclusion of collective action clauses in all international sovereign bonds would represent an important improvement in the international financial architecture',[83] and this is because it would remove the ability to issue bonds away from the possibility of CACs which some countries may do to appeal to particular creditors who would not want to be bound the majority of creditors within a particular bond offering.

The main difference between a CAC and the SDRM was that in a CAC, voting on the procedure and the way to treat a particular issue are done on a series-by-series basis. The SDRM, in contrast, proposed to aggregate voting across all debt instruments covered in the restructuring process.[84] In simple terms, a CAC affects one particular instrument or loan that creditors may have subscribed to, but the SDRM considers the debtor's position as an aggregate, and *all* the creditors who are related to that debtor will be impacted by the debt treatment decision taken by the majority of creditors across the board.

However, whilst the details could always be altered and configured to suit the situation better, there was one particular element that would prove crucial to the chances of the IMF getting the SDRM plan through: its own constitution. Whilst the IMF has, today, 190 members, its internal voting structure on the direction of the IMF means that one country, in particular, holds sway. The US has nearly three times the voting power of the next member – Japan – and has a track record of using this influence to its advantage. In the case of the SDRM, when the idea was put forward, it was the US and its allies that voted against the plan.[85] From a strategic viewpoint, this could have been because of a difference of opinion on the best model to aid with debt restructurings, the primacy of the US with regards to CACs, or a more sinister standpoint that equates to not wanting to help vulnerable countries *too* much. However, many developing countries voted against the proposal too, and Setser suggests this was because of a fear that centralising this system would reduce the availability of IMF-backed loans. On the other side, a large number of European countries supported the mechanism because of the idea that it would reduce IMF 'bailouts', which was a distinct aim of the SDRM. Nevertheless, the reality is that the SDRM did not make it past its own threshold. The geo-political landscape is something that clouds the multilateral institutions' attempts to provide for debt treatment, and we shall see that in the coming chapters. As the western world unknowingly hurtled towards the Financial Crisis, Africa was about to enter its next stage of debt treatment, and this one would lead to a host of unintended consequences.

1.8 The Multilateral Debt Relief Initiative 2006

The Multilateral Debt Relief Initiative (MDRI) and the Heavily Indebted Poor Countries Initiative (HIPC) have been separated in the chapter, but one should not think of them as being entirely independent of one another. In reality, the MDRI represents the global community's attempt to lift poorer countries out of dependency for good, building on the developments of the HIPC just a decade earlier.[86] The aim, in a nutshell, was to provide particular countries with irrevocable debt relief within sectors where the debt burden was heaviest. The strategic aim of the initiative was to solidify the gains that had been seen via the structural adjustment programmes that had been implemented via the HIPC initiative.[87] We shall see that there were successes that the global community could point to for years to come but that, ultimately, the timing and the changing nature of the global financial environment would lead to some dire consequences in the years to come.

Explaining the MDRI is quite simple, and the IMF sum everything up quite neatly:

> In 2005, the help accelerate progress toward the United Nations Millennium Development Goals, the HIPC initiative was supplemented by the Multilateral Debt Relief Initiative. The MDRI allows for 100 percent relief on eligible debts by three multilateral institutions – the IMF, the World Bank, and the African Development Fund – for countries completing the HIPC initiative process.[88]

In terms of 'completing the HIPC initiative process', the IMF mean here the two-step process we looked at when reviewing the HIPC initiative. Thus, those eligible for full relief were the countries that had joined the HIPC and come through both the 'decision point' and 'completion point' stages of the HIPC initiative. Though the G-8 had pushed for the above, the IMF extended eligibility to *any* country that had a per capita income of $380 or less instead of just those that had gone through the HIPC initiative, although this only captured a few more countries.[89]

The aim of the MDRI was to capture the elements of the debt landscape that had previously gone untouched. Many vulnerable countries owed the majority of the debt to the multilateral institutions; thus, the MDRI sought to capture that element and fundamentally remove it from the equation. The multilateral institutions, especially the World Bank, often make the point that reducing their debt is unwise because it reduces their capability to intervene elsewhere, but the political pressure coming from the G-8 pushed the multilateral institutions into unchartered territory. The UK, who were pushing the hardest for the MDRI to be developed, argued that donors should be the ones to shoulder the responsibility and, essentially, take the financial hit for the debt relief. The US argued against this and pushed for the institutions themselves to take a financial hit. Whilst the EU argued for an amendment to the HIPC thresholds to generate more funds, it was the US and the UK who came to a compromise that saw the affected multilateral development banks have their losses eased by the donors and the IMF utilise its internal resources to cushion the financial blow from providing wide-ranging debt relief.[90]

The MDRI was greeted as a radical development in the field of debt treatment. As Moss explains, 'the MDRI achieves what debt campaigners might have thought impossible just a few years ago: close to full debt relief for some of the world's poorest countries'. However, Moss explains that not everything was perfect when the initiative was launched because 'although this is being presented as a momentous leap forward for Africa and the battle against global poverty, the actual gains may be more modest and elusive. Hopes for a transformative impact on poverty – or even a meaningful effect on the cash flow of African treasuries – are unlikely to be realised. This does not imply that the MDRI is meaningless, but rather that the potential benefits are far from certain, likely to be long-term, and are not of the kind that many activists or observers may be expecting'.[91] Writing in the same year that the MDRI was launched, one can understand Moss's concerns. However, in hindsight, the initiative was more successful than Moss predicted.

For example, just six years after implementation, 'the median public debt level (as a percent of GDP) for sub-Saharan Africa declined to about 31 percent in 2012, far below the levels leading up to the HIPC initiative'.[92] By 2009, 26 countries had reached the completion point and qualified for irrevocable debt relief from the multilateral institutions, and whilst $45 billion had been committed to post-decision point countries via the MDRI,[93] the eventual total was just over $41 billion, with the total amount of debt relieved by both the HIPC and MDRI initiatives coming in at just over $116 billion.[94]

However, everything must have a consequence, and the actions taken in the name of the MDRI are no different. There were concerns raised at the time regarding the concept of a 'moral hazard', in that the cleaning of the countries' balance sheets will open them up to new debt – which is not necessarily a bad thing – but that the new debt would be attained whilst the countries were still struggling with governance issues and fiscal indiscipline.[95] As Coulibaly et al. mention, unless there were impactful reforms, the fear was that history would repeat itself. In addition, the newfound financial space that was provided via the MDRI meant the countries who had benefited were now hurtling towards a post-Financial Crisis era that was dominated by large capital market players hungry for any sort of yield in a repressed global environment. The need to borrow remained for the sovereign states, and the rates of interest that they had to pay to gain that investment became increasingly attractive to the capital markets despite all of the risks that came with such investments. Once again, Africa was to be impacted by the global financial environment, and it was not prepared.

1.9 Conclusion

The history of debt treatment within the African continent is a complicated one. It becomes clearer when seen through the lens of the legacy of colonialism and the ideological foundation of neo-colonialism. The mistakes made in early debt treatment initiatives where the approach was to 'end' debt dependency were costly. The money and resources provided for such initiatives were sometimes extraordinary, but the result was the same every time. This calls into question the wisdom of those designing such treatments.

One of the most important aspects of this chapter has been to acknowledge the importance of the *environment* in the concept of indebtedness. The changing nature of the financial environment is something that needed to be considered when developing debt treatment initiatives, but this was not always the case. The knock-on effects of any intervention are vitally important to understand, but this issue was ignored time and time again as we saw throughout the chapter. However, it is perhaps more important now than ever as we shall delve much deeper in the remaining chapters. This is because the 'changing of the guard', so to speak, in that private creditors (for reasons we shall explore next) have been elevated into being the predominant lenders to the African continent, brings with it an array of problems. Whilst many theoreticians cited in this chapter were absolutely correct to play down the effects of elements such as collective action problems because, at their time of writing, private creditors were not as prevalent in the debt picture, we have no such luxury today. We shall see that the major issue today is exactly what had been played down. We may question whether the idea of the SDRM would be seen differently in today's light as the financial environment has changed so much, but the reality is that vulnerable countries are now being left to the mercy of the market without adequate protection. The reasons for not implementing something much more formal in terms of debtor protection may be many, but the fact of the matter is that fundamental problems within the creditor/debtor relationship are now being played out on the global level.

We saw how it took almost forty years for the global community to finally understand that debt revocation was the only way forward, and as we shall see shortly even that did not work for long. Now, we are in a position where the rules of the game have changed dramatically with the inclusion of private creditors who bring with them many different practices and controlling sentiments, such as the reality that the majority of private creditors are investors investing on behalf of collectives and, therefore, have fiduciary duties which make their options for flexibility that much more limited. All of this is impactful, but when we include the credit rating agencies into the picture, the complexity is ratcheted up many more levels. Every time these fundamental dynamics are being played out, citizens in affected countries go without basic infrastructure and, as a result, many are being exposed to political and militaristic struggles which will leave a lasting mark. Hopefully, as the reader, you can now understand why the book is aiming to shine a light on the underlying and structural dynamics of this issue, an issue of finance, society, history, and humankind.

Notes

1 Anne O. Krueger, *A New Approach to Sovereign Debt Restructuring* (International Monetary Fund 2002) 40.

2 For example, see Robert Harms, *Land of Tears: The Exploration and Exploitation of Equatorial Africa* (Hachette 2019); Joseph Hodge, Gerald Hold, and Martina Kopf (eds), *Developing Africa: Concepts and Practices in Twentieth-Century Colonialism* (Manchester University Press 2016); A. Adu Boahen, *African Perspectives on European Colonialism*

(Diasporic Africa Press 2011); and L.H. Gann, Peter Duignan, and Victor Witter Turner (eds), *Colonialism in Africa 1870–1960: Volume 4* (CUP 1969).

3 Walter Rodney, *How Europe Underdeveloped Africa* (Verso 2018) 86.

4 Ibid 87.

5 Ibid 107.

6 Ibid 115.

7 Thomas Peakenham, *The Scramble for Africa* (Hachette 2015).

8 Ibid 2.

9 Jonathan Rosa and Nelson Flores, 'Reimagining Race and Language: From Raciolinguistic Ideologies to a Raciolinguistic Perspective' in H. Samy Alim, Angela Reyes, and Paul V. Kroskrity, *The Oxford Handbook of Language and Race* (OUP 2020) 93: 'nation-state/colonial governmentality relied on raciolinguistic ideologies that positioned colonised populations as inferior to idealised European populations. In the early period of European colonialism of the Americas, these raciolinguistic ideologies positioned Indigenous American and enslaved African populations as sub-human.

10 Godfrey Mwakikagile, *Africa after Independence: Realities of Nationhood with Photos* (New Africa Press 2006) 81.

11 Between 1910 and 1958, a total of 12 countries became independent from their colonial masters, including Egypt, Libya, and South Africa from the British, and Morocco, Tunisia, and Guinea from the French. See Alistair Boddy-Evans, 'Chronological List of African Independence' (2020) *ThoughtCo.* (Jan 25) www.thoughtco.com/chronological-list-of-african-independence-4070467.

12 Ibid.

13 Mwakikagile (n 10) 81.

14 European Union, 'History of the European Union 1960–69' (2022) *European Union* (Jan 14) https://european-union.europa.eu/principles-countries-history/history-eu/1960-69_en.

15 Peo Hansen and Stefan Jonsson, *Eurafrica: The Untold History of European Integration and Colonialism* (Bloomsbury Publishing 2014) 8.

16 Ibid 11.

17 Ibid 27.

18 Ibid 28.

19 J. Shola Omotola and Hassan Saliu, 'Foreign Aid, Debt Relief and Africa's Debt Development: Problems and Prospects' (2009) 16 *South African Journal of International Affairs* 1 87–102, 87.

20 Gregoire Mallard, 'We Owe You Nothing: Decolonisation and Sovereign Debt Obligations in International Public Law' in Pierre Penet and Juan Flores Zendejas, *Sovereign Debt Diplomacies: Rethinking Sovereign Debt from Colonial Empires to Hegemony* (OUP 2021) 189. For more on the concept of the NIEO, see an array of viewpoints within Karl P. Sauvant and Hajo Hasenpflug, *The New International Economic Order: Confrontation or Cooperation Between North and South?* (Routledge 2019).

21 Leigh Gardner, 'Colonialism or Supersanctions: Sovereignty and Debt in West Africa, 1871–1914' (2017) 21 *European Review of Economic History* 236–257, 236.

22 Ibid 239.

23 Mallard (n 20) 190.

24 Omotola and Saliu (n 19) 91.

25 Mallard (n 20) 190.

26 Boris Gamarra, Malvina Pollock, and Carlos A. Primo Braga, 'Debt Relief to Low-Income Countries: A Retrospective' in Dörte Dömeland and Carlos A. Primo Braga, *Debt Relief and Beyond* (The World Bank 2009) 12.

27 Michael Rauscher, *OPEC and the Price of Petroleum: Theoretical Considerations and Empirical Evidence* (Springer 2012) 26.

28 Willard R. Johnson and Ernest J. Wilson, 'The "Oil Crises" and African Economies: Oil Wave on a Tidal Flood of Industrial Price Inflation' (1982) 111 *Daedalus* 2, 211–241, 211.

29 Ibid 211.
30 Joan Chaker, *Debt as Colonialism* (Progressive International 2021).
31 Ibid.
32 Development Reimagined, *Options for Reimagining Africa's Debt System* (2021) https://heyzine.com/flip-book/981ad6e913.html#page/1 19.
33 Chaker (n 30).
34 David Roodman 'Credit Initiatives in the 1980s and 1990s' in Chris Jochnick and Fraser A. Preston, *Sovereign Debt at the Crossroads: Challenges and Proposals for Resolving the Third World Debt Crisis* (OUP 2006) 13.
35 Alemayehu G. Fole, 'The Historical Origin of African Debt Crisis' (2002) 19 *Eastern Africa Social Science Research Review* 1 59–89, 60.
36 Ibid.
37 Roodman (n 34) 19.
38 Gamarra et al. (n 26).
39 Ibid.
40 Ibid 14.
41 Ibid.
42 Ibid 15.
43 Ibid.
44 Roodman (n 34) 15.
45 South African Reserve Bank, 'An Opening Address by Lesetja Kganyago, Governor of the South African Reserve Bank, at the Fourth Annual Distributed Sovereign Debt Research and Management Conference' (2020) www.bis.org/review/r200910b.pdf 6.
46 IMF, 'Debt Relief Under the Heavily Indebted Poor Countries (HIPC) Initiative' (2021) www.imf.org/en/About/Factsheets/Sheets/2016/08/01/16/11/Debt-Relief-Under-the-Heavily-Indebted-Poor-Countries-Initiative.
47 Fole (n 35) 70.
48 IMF (n 46).
49 Madhur Gautam, *Debt Relief for the Poorest: An OED Review of the HIPC Initiative* (World Bank Publications 2003) ix.
50 Michael Edwards, 'Introduction' in Michael Edwards, *The Oxford Handbook of Civil Society* (OUP 2013) 3.
51 World Economic Forum, *The Future Role of Civil Society* (2013) http://www3.weforum.org/docs/WEF_FutureRoleCivilSociety_Report_2013.pdf.
52 IMF, 'The Enhanced Initiative for Heavily Indebted Poor Countries – Review of Implementation' (2000) *IMF* (Sep 7) www.imf.org/external/np/hipc/2000/ehipc.htm#I.
53 Gautam (n 49) xiii.
54 Shonar Lala, Rupa Ranganathan, and Brett Libresco, *Debt Relief for the Poorest: An Evaluation Update of the HIPC Initiative* (World Bank Publications 2006) xiii.
55 IMF (n 46).
56 Ibid.
57 Gamarra et al. (n 26) 27.
58 Martin Dent and Bill Peters, *The Crisis of Poverty and Debt in the Third World* (Routledge 2019).
59 Ann Pettifor, 'The Jubilee 2000 Campaign: A Brief Overview' in Chris Jochnick and Fraser A. Preston, *Sovereign Debt at the Crossroads: Challenges and Proposals for Resolving the Third World Debt Crisis* (OUP 2006) 299.
60 Ibid.
61 Marjorie Mayo, *Global Citizens: Social Movements and the Challenge of Globalisation* (Zed Books 2005) 173.
62 Pettifor (n 59).
63 Advocacy International, 'Jubilee 2000' (2021) *Advocacy International* (Jan 17) www.advocacyinternational.co.uk/featured-project/jubilee-2000#:~:text=Jubilee%202000%20was%20a%20global,35%20of%20the%20poorest%20countries.

64 Nancy Birdsall, John Williamson, and Brian Deese, *Delivering on Debt Relief: From IMF Gold to a New Aid Architecture* (Peterson Institute 2002) 1.
65 Joshua W. Busby, 'Bono Made Jesse Helms Cry: Jubilee 2000, Debt Relief, and Moral Action in International Politics' (2007) 51 *International Studies Quarterly* 247–275, 250.
66 Helen Yanacopulos, 'The Public Face of Debt' (2004) 16 *Journal of International Development* 717–727, 717.
67 Nick Buxton, 'Debt Cancellation and Civil Society: A Case Study of Jubilee 2000' in Paul Gready, *Fighting for Human Rights* (Routledge 2004) 54.
68 Mayo (n 61) 174.
69 Christopher Oechsli, 'Procedural Guidelines for Renegotiating LDC Debts: An Analogy to Chapter 11 of the U.S. Bankruptcy Reform Act' (1981) 21 *Virginia Journal of International Law* 2 305–341.
70 Kenneth Rogoff and Jeromin Zettelmeyer, 'Bankruptcy Procedures for Sovereigns: A History of Ideas, 1976–2001' (2002) 49 *IMF Staff Papers* 3 470–507, 472.
71 Ibid 473.
72 For Cohen's work on a statutory model, see Benjamin Cohen, *Developing Country Debt: A Middle Way* (Princeton University Press 1989).
73 Richard Euliss, 'The Feasibility of the IMF's Sovereign Debt Restructuring Mechanism; An Alternative Statutory Approach to Mollify American Reservations' (2003) 19 *American University International Law Review* 1, 115.
74 Rogoff and Zettelmeyer (n 70) 490.
75 Krueger (n 1).
76 Ibid 4.
77 Euliss (n 73) 115.
78 World Bank, *Global Development Finance: Striving for Stability in Development Finance* (World Bank 2003) 64.
79 Ibid.
80 Ibid 66.
81 Ibid.
82 Krueger (n 1) 7.
83 Ibid 29.
84 IMF, *Sovereign Debt Restructuring – Recent Developments and Implications for the Fund's Legal and Policy Framework* (2013) www.imf.org/external/np/pp/eng/2013/042613.pdf 14.
85 Brad Setser, 'The Political Economy of the SDRM' in Barry Herman, Jose Antonio Ocampo, and Shari Spiegel, *Overcoming Developing Country Debt Crises* (OUP 2010).
86 Abdoul G. Mijiyawa, 'External Debt in Developing Countries Since HIPC and MDRI: What are the Driving Factors?' (2020) *International Journal of Finance & Economics* 1–17, 1.
87 Jacinta Nwachukwu, 'The Prospects for Foreign Debt Sustainability in Post-Completion-Point Countries: Implications of the HIPC-MDRI Framework' (2008) 26 *Development Policy Review* 2 171–188, 171.
88 IMF (n 46).
89 IMF, *Multilateral Debt Relief Initiative – Questions and Answers* (2017) www.imf.org/external/np/exr/mdri/eng/index.htm.
90 Martin A. Weiss, *The Multilateral Debt Relief Initiative* (Congressional Research Service 2012) 4.
91 Todd Moss, 'Will Debt Relief Make a Difference? Impact and Expectations of the Multilateral Debt Relief Initiative' (2006) *Centre for Global Development: Working Paper* #88, 3.
92 Brahima S. Coulibaly, Dhruv Gandhi, and Lemma W. Senbet, 'Is sub-Saharan Africa Facing Another Systemic Sovereign Debt Crisis?' (2019) *Africa Growth Initiative at Brookings: Policy Brief.* www.brookings.edu/wp-content/uploads/2019/04/africa_sovereign_debt_sustainability.pdf 1.
93 Gamarra et al. (n 26) 29.
94 World Bank, *Annual Meetings 2014* (2014) www.worldbank.org/content/dam/Worldbank/Feature%20Story/Debt/HIPC_Fall2014_ENG_CRA_web.pdf.
95 Coulibaly et al. (n 92) 2.

2 The Impact of the COVID-19 Pandemic

2.1 Introduction

The aim of this chapter is two-fold: on one hand, we need to continue our genealogical 'story' so that we can conclude with what needs to happen as the continent moves forward (or at least be able to suggest potential developments); on the other hand, we need to deviate (relatively speaking) and focus on the humanist impact of the global pandemic. It is a vital part of the story that often gets overlooked in the financially concerned literature, as if the two are not connected. They are, and if the financial system is leading directly to human suffering, misery, and death, then this understanding needs to be put at the very forefront of every analysis undertaken. In this chapter, we shall be doing exactly that.

It is also the aim to paint a picture of how the environment we witness today led to what I call the 'credit rating impasse'. As we saw in the last chapter, this concept of environment is something we cannot relegate to mere circumstance. Several important elements occurred once the multilateral institutions had sought to essentially clear the balance sheets of the world's most vulnerable and, as a result, the well-meaning initiatives of the mid-2000s have made the countries more vulnerable than ever before in the post-Independence era.

To be abundantly clear, this approach is not about blame. The pandemic the world is experiencing is not the doing of the financial system. The question here though is what role does the financial system play, if any, in aiding society in its time of need? What role does it play in aiding *human beings*. Whilst there may be people who advance the argument that it is not the financial system's role to aid wider society, I would choose to disregard that solely on the basis that the modern financial system is quick to seek societal help when things go wrong, mostly under the banner of negative effect upon society if that assistance is not given; if it is the case that the financial system, therefore, cannot help aid human survival, then this is negative, and if it would be negative not to save the financial system when it fails, then we are faced with a purely negative entity. Again, it is purely a belief, but I do not choose to believe that the financial system *cannot* aid those suffering from the deadly pandemic, or that it *will not* which is a much worse charge; perhaps, it is the case that it does not

DOI: 10.4324/9781003261223-3

have the capability to. If we believe this, then we must also believe that one's capability can be changed and improved, and that is what this book focuses on. That connection between systemic capability and human survival is fundamental, but first, we must understand more about how human beings are directly suffering at the hands of the pandemic *before* we get to how the financial system is compounding such misery.

2.2 The Non-Financial Impact of the COVID-19 Pandemic

My first inclination when deciding on the title for this section was to call it 'The Human Impact of the COVID-19 Pandemic', but this would not have been accurate because all of the impacts coming from the pandemic, whether financial or non-financial, will end up affecting human beings in one way or another. Thus, to start the chapter's analyses, there is a need to assess how the pandemic has impacted the African continent in terms of health, politics, and societal structure before we start to analyse the effects on debt and the ability to provide resources. We shall see, however, in line with my sentiment at the start of this paragraph, that the two are intrinsically interlinked and that is, in effect, the whole point of this book: the *consequence* of being unable to focus on channelling resources into key health and societal infrastructures because of debt and debt servicing burdens is, inevitably, a consequence that citizens must face.

In continuing the crucial caveat made at the beginning of the book, it is important to reiterate here that Africa is a continent made up of very different countries, regions, and peoples. The UN articulate this important point well:

> Moreover, as with other regions, there is not one homogenous narrative around the COVID-19 pandemic in Africa. The pandemic is affecting African countries differently, given varied strengths and vulnerabilities. Only one third of Africans have access to proper hand washing, for instance, and there is less than one doctor per one thousand people on the continent. But some countries also have a wealth of relevant lessons from dealing with previous HIV/AIDS and Ebola epidemics on engaging communities, communicating risks and adapting local and innovative methods to craft African approaches to control spread of the disease.[1]

We shall see that contrasting experience and capability discussed time and time again as we continue because when we look at financial impacts next, we shall see that the northern and southern parts of the continent were worse affected financially.[2] In sub-Saharan Africa (SSA), where one may expect case numbers to be particularly high (especially at the beginning of the pandemic), the statistics that were being shared told a different story.

After the continent confirmed its first case in early February 2020 (in Egypt), only three months later, the continent-wide statistics started to be revealed and were relatively modest. Frimpong et al. tell us that by April 2020, there were just under 20,000 confirmed cases and just over 1000 confirmed fatalities. However, given the transmissibility of the virus, it is not surprising that the scholars then tell us that 'having gone nearly 100 days before reaching 100,000 cases, it took the continent only 18 more days to reach 200,000 cases'.[3] Early data also confirmed trends that would be maintained throughout the pandemic. For example, in the rural villages in SSA, where about 60% of the SSA population live, there was an alarming rise in COVID-19 contraction. This was because 'Africa's rural communities tend to lack basic public amenities such as healthcare, roads, water, education, and effective local governance. In particular, their weak healthcare infrastructure increases the risk of COVID-19 among rural populations'.[4]

However, as employment opportunities grind to a halt because of the pandemic, there is an increased need for rural–urban migration for employment. This means that the urban centres are equally affected. Because 'Africa's slums and urban communities are over-crowded and suffer from poor sanitation, acute water shortage, and other inadequacies in basic social services',[5] the virus spread like wildfire. Yet, whilst developed regions and economies were shutting down, the rates on the African continent were relatively low.[6] This led to headlines such as 'The pandemic appears to have spared Africa so far. Scientists are struggling to explain why',[7] which has had the unfortunate consequence of breeding complacency at the global level. Early on in the pandemic, the WHO recognised Africa as the least affected region globally, stating that the continent's experience only translated to 1.5% of the world's impact from COVID-19.[8] Several potential reasons were given for this, ranging from the comparatively younger population of the continent to the climate. However, as we shall see shortly, there were much more pertinent reasons as to why the case numbers were, comparatively, so low.

However, before that, the second, third, and fourth waves of the COVID-19 pandemic reveal a steadily worsening situation for the continent. The second wave began to take hold towards the end of 2020, and in early 2021, the WHO reported that 'deaths from COVID-19 in Africa have surged by 40% in the last month, pushing Africa's death toll towards 100,000 since the first reported case on the continent'.[9] Researchers who performed cross-sectional studies revealed the rate of increase; by the end of 2020, the 1.5% share of the global impact had risen to 3.6%; revealingly, nine out of 55 countries on the continent accounted for more than 82% of the cases, which was put down to the urban centres that were drawing people in for employment. The third wave saw the impact of vaccination represented in the figures, according to the WHO.[10] Whilst vaccination access/distribution and 'vaccine apartheid'[11] are extraordinarily important and impactful issues, in August 2021, the WHO said that 13 million doses had been taken on the continent and that this was contributing to a 'stabilisation' of the spread. With 1.3 billion people on the continent, 13 million is certainly not a lot. The fourth wave, mostly driven by the Omicron variant, was identified in and mostly affected South Africa, with the rest of the continent showing much lower cases and deaths than other parts of the world.[12]

This whistle-stop account of the four different waves that have impacted the African continent was meant to provide context for some underlying aspects that deserve attention. The low numbers being displayed for the rest of the world to see were, on occasion, being used to justify a lack of help from more developed regions, especially when it came to vaccine sharing and distribution. However, there is so much doubt cast on the accuracy of the said statistics that they almost become meaningless. For example, researchers from the British Medical Journal (BMJ) found that the 'impact of COVID-19 in Africa has been vastly underestimated' and that 'the findings shows that covid-19 deaths accounted for 15–20% of all sampled deaths – many more than official reports suggest and contradicting the widely held view that covid-19 has largely skipped Africa and had little impact'.[13] Maula puts it even more simply: 'inadequate health statistics information systems need to be considered when assessing the infection and mortality rates'.[14] This lack of capability can have a tremendously impactful effect on perceptions of the ability to defend against the pandemic, but the reality of that health information system capability is stark:

> only one in seven Covid-19 infections in Africa are being detected, meaning the continent's estimated infection level may be 59 million people, according to a new study by the World Health Organisation. 'With limited testing, we're flying blind in far too many communities in Africa', said Matshidiso Moeti, regional director for the WHO in Africa.[15]

Even the WHO's understanding of the impact on lesser testing capabilities is only an estimate, meaning the real rate of infection could be much greater on the continent.

It would stand to reason, if not just pure common sense, that regions such as Africa (in particular, certain parts of Africa) would struggle to hold back the COVID-19 wave. Even just on a purely economic understanding, the lack of ability to 'lock down', provide everybody who needs personal protection equipment (PPE) with it, or essentially disincentivise people from mixing together for employment purposes with initiatives such as 'furlough' or 'stimulus cheques' and the subsequent effects when battling a highlight contagious virus should have been clear to anybody who cared, but that was not the case. In the era of hyper-competitive vaccine-based nationalism, the statistics that suggested Africa was handling things quite well, all considered, led to the view in parts that 'after all, if there are relatively few cases and deaths, then some people may say, "Good, no problem – they don't need vaccines"'.[16] Sarah Wild included this in her article, within which she also includes the findings of Dr Maysoon Dahab, who found that, as just one example, 'only 2 percent of COVID deaths in Khartoum, Sudan, were correctly attributed to the illness between last April and September (2020)'. The effect of this is staggering because not only are people not being tested and diagnosed correctly but even after death are being miscategorised because of a technical and economic inability to conduct the proper testing procedures.

There is more evidence of underreporting across the continent, and the more advanced economies on the continent are reporting much higher numbers than elsewhere. For example, South Africa and Morocco have been consistently amongst those reporting the highest figures on the continent, but their testing systems and healthcare infrastructures are much more advanced than other regions on the continent.[17] Furthermore, their death-related statistics are higher than the majority of the continent; again, this is due to more advanced health information systems. However, even in the more developed economies on the continent, evidence is rife regarding underreporting. Nigeria, the most populous country on the continent, has *never* reported more than five infections per 100,000. This remarkably low rate of infection that was officially recorded was put to the test by researchers, and after conducting a study based on blood samples collected from citizens in Lagos, the study concluded that at least 23% had been infected. This implies that 'official case numbers substantially underestimated the actual infection rates'.[18]

There is a range of impacts emanating from the COVID-19 pandemic in Africa. One, which is related to this chronic rate of underreporting, is that the low statistics are contributing to a vicious cycle. As Wild describes:

> But if reported COVID cases are low, officials may struggle to persuade people to get a shot even if they are in a position to do so. The low reported disease numbers are bolstering vaccine hesitancy, warns Catherine Kyobutungi, executive director of the African Population and Health Research Center in Nairobi, Kenya. 'People are asking why they need to be vaccinated when they've already gotten rid of the virus without vaccines,' she says.
>
> Without widespread access to vaccines, African countries are relying on basic public health measures such as mask wearing and handwashing alone to control the disease's spread. And, as with vaccination, people could dismiss these measures as unnecessary if the numbers misrepresent the risk of infection.[19]

This vicious cycle is already affecting deeper underlying problems in many countries, with it being simply suggested that 'the pandemic has exacerbated health system challenges in many African countries'[20] and that, tragically, 'health workers and health systems in Africa are dangerously overstretched'.[21]

Whilst the UN plans to increase testing capabilities on the continent and planned to test more than 7 million people before the end of 2021, the reality of the impact on public health does not make for comfortable reading for anybody involved. The UN estimated in a report that 'approximately 600 million Africans live in urban areas, of which 56 percent live in slums'. Further, 'many African urban households live in a single room, do not have potable water, or reside in overcrowded neighbourhoods. Only 34 percent of the African population has access to handwashing facilities'. On a basic hygiene level, the continent was statistically at the mercy of the virus, but there are additional aspects to consider. As the UN continue, 'weak health systems and the prevalence of underlying health conditions, such as HIV/AIDS, tuberculosis, malaria, and malnutrition, as well as challenges to state authority from armed groups, render parts of the continent particularly suspectable to contagion'. Add to this environment the fact that there was, is, and will likely continue to be a limited amount of PPE available to African countries as other countries have only recently dropped their restrictions on exporting PPE, then the potential for devastation is abundantly clear.[22]

The paragraphs above reveal an even bleaker picture. In relation to malnutrition, it is widely anticipated that food insecurity on the continent will endure through the pandemic and beyond.[23] The African continent was working towards meeting ambitious and much-needed goals, such as those contained within the Sustainable Development Goals (SDG) but, as Maula argues, 'the pandemic will impact and delay the realisation of most the gender relevant SDG targets'. Furthermore, 'targets related to women's economic participation and empowerment, youth unemployment, education, maternal and child health, sexual reproductive health, child marriage, gender-based violence, and female genital mutilation are most likely to be affected negatively.[24] Ameyaw et al. continue this understanding:

> Reproductive healthcare is one of the core aspects that has been severely threatened. This is critical considering the limited utilisation of essential maternal health services due to pre-existing systemic barriers faced by African women in their quest to access antenatal care (ANC), facility-based childbirth and family planning services. For instance, Adedokun and Yaya using Demographic and Health Survey (DHS) data from 31 African countries, noted that 13% of the women did not utilise ANC at all, whilst 35% utilised ANC services partially. Another study of 28 African countries based on DHS data revealed that facility-based childbirth ranges from 23% with an average of 66%. In terms of prevalence and maternal health impact of COVID-19 in Africa, the worst affected countries include South Africa, where a 3.4% rise in perinatal mortality and 5% decline in family planning services has occurred due to COVID-19. Others are Liberia, Uganda, Zambia, and the Democratic Republic of Congo. In spite of these, COVID-19 measures were instituted in a number of African countries such as South Africa, Kenya, Ghana and Africa at large have extensively focused on how to cushion the citizens from the downturns in earnings and other similar measures to revamp the economy. Workable interventions to sustain and potentially even improve the ailing reproductive health system have been largely omitted in COVID-19 measures in Africa. This affirms the prediction by the United Nations Population Fund (UNFPA) that during crises, reproductive health needs are likely to be overlooked.[25]

In relation to the pandemic's effect on the long-standing health issues in the community, Holtz describes the impact clearly. Globally, in 2020, access to healthcare decreased significantly, which Holtz suggests was both down to patient-based hesitancy (i.e. not wanting to contract the virus) and from the provider's perspective, large-scale mandates to prioritise the treatment of COVID-19 above other issues. This also caused health information campaigns to be relegated as the focus was on COVID-19, which again Holtz points to as contributing to a reduction in access to healthcare services. In relation to tuberculosis, Holtz notes a 60% decline in diagnosis and an 80% decline in referrals. For malaria, Holtz notes a sharp decline in malaria treatment in Africa, which is very worrying indeed when we remember that malaria is still endemic in Africa; the continent makes up nearly 94% of the world's cases and death statistics.[26]

However, it is not just physical and mental health that has been on the front line. As we shall see in Chapter 4, the political foundations across the African continent are of the utmost importance to the geo-political landscape. On that front, the pandemic has been particularly impactful. Frimpong et al. discuss how 'some African regimes have made notable attempts to instrumentalise COVID-19 to perpetuate their incumbency. Eighteen African countries were scheduled to hold elections in 2020; only six have conducted their polls so far'.[27] As the UN Secretary-General said in his end-of-term speech at the end of 2021:

> Meanwhile, inequalities keep widening. Social upheaval and polarisation will be growing. And the risks keep increasing. This is a powder keg for social unrest and instability. It poses a clear and present danger to democratic institutions.[28]

Frimpong et al. comment on this aspect and confirm that 'some incumbents are using COVID-19 as a reason to curtail campaign activities of opposition parties'. In continuation, Agwanda et al. fear much more in this respect, and with particular reference to certain parts of the continent:

> But of more concern were the potential indirect political consequences of the virus. Although SSA has made great strides economically, the continent still has struggled with endemic problems of political instability, human rights violations, corruption, conflicts, humanitarian crises, unfair electoral processes, and weak governance. The public health measures and protocols that were needed to manage the further spread of the virus could be easily exploited by autocratic regimes to centralize political power.[29]

There are many impacts of the COVID-19 pandemic on the African continent. There is ample evidence to suggest that we can confidently dismiss the majority of the official records that tell us the pandemic has not had Africa in its grip; it has. However, it is argued here that all of those impacts and the inability to adequately address them are connected. They are connected by the concept of shortage. That shortage, in a great part, comes from the diversion of much-needed resources from social and healthcare spending into the servicing and payments of debt. This book does not call for debt cancellation but instead calls for *adequate* debt restructuring in the sovereign's interest, not the creditors', or, rather amazingly when articulated, the *freedom to restructure with private creditors.* Sovereign states, in representing their citizenry, must be allowed to restructure their debts with their creditors to provide the fiscal space to recover, but the credit rating impasse is preventing that from happening. In this first section of the chapter, we have seen the *human* impact of the pandemic and how it has transformed the continent's future. Next, we shall examine the *economic* impact of the pandemic, with all of this analysis building up to the articulation of the credit rating impasse and how it is preventing the continent from recovering as quickly as it should.

2.3 The Financial Impact of the COVID-19 Pandemic

This chapter has already dealt with aspects of the pandemic that can be, in a way, painted as economic problems. For example, increased economic migration from the rural villages to the urban centres will have economic effects on the country in question, as too will diverting precious resources away from deep-rooted healthcare problems and towards COVID-19 treatment, potentially affecting those employed or employable. However, there are structural economic impacts that have pushed the continent into the position it is in.

In our linear story, the last round of debt treatment – the MDRI – sought to clear the debts of countries with regards to multilateral debt. As one of the largest proportions of the debt held by African countries, the effect of the MDRI was to clear substantial space on the balance sheets of many vulnerable countries. In the time between the MDRI and the COVID-19 pandemic, two things happened. First, the countries in receipt of the relief utilised the fiscal space relatively well and adopted several policies, as part of the relief deals, that gave some cause for optimism on the continent. This was certainly a positive outcome from the MDRI. However, there are often unintended consequences to a decision, and the MDRI neatly fits into that category. The IMF and World Bank made no secret about wanting to remove themselves from the debt cycle problem and lessen their burden. While the multilateral institutions effectively cleared the balance sheets of many countries, the western world was hurtling towards the Financial Crisis. After a few years of painful economic recession, investors returned to the scene *needing* to invest their resources (holding onto resources too long is extremely negative for many large investors) and, when surveying the global environment for investment opportunities, the sovereign debt of vulnerable countries began to look appealing. The yields connected to the country's debt offerings managed to entice investors trapped within a post-Financial Crisis low-yield environment. Something to note here is that the credit rating agencies had warned the investors of the risks of investing in vulnerable, often fragile countries, with their very low ratings, but this did not deter them.

This is why it is widely acknowledged that the continent was performing relatively well before the pandemic struck, which makes the current situation so difficult to accept. As the UN confirmed in a report:

> The COVID-19 pandemic arrived at a moment when prospects for many African countries were promising. At the beginning of 2020, Africa was on track to continue its economic expansion, with growth projected to rise from 2.9 per cent in 2019 to 3.2 per cent in 2020, and 3.5 per cent in 2021. Important gains were being registered in poverty reduction and health indicators. Technology and innovation were being increasingly embraced across the continent, with young Africans acting as early adopters of new platforms such as mobile money.

Furthermore:

> Progress had also been made with respect to political unity and economic integration. The entry into force of the African Continental Free Trade Area (AfCFTA) in May 2019 promised to boost intra-African trade by as much as 25 per cent by 2040. Furthermore, Africa enjoyed some of the highest global returns on foreign direct investment (FDI). Several inclusive elections, increasingly the norm for a majority of African countries, were due to be held in 2020.[30]

Agwanda et al. note similar statistics and add that 'significant gains were also recorded in health indicators and poverty reduction'.[31]

However, even before the pandemic reached African shores, the gains mentioned above began to reverse, and quickly. The UN confirmed that the major factors were the falling demand for Africa's commodities, capital flight, a virtual collapse of tourism and air transportation, and a depreciation of local currencies as a result of a deterioration in the current account balance.[32] Nobody on the continent could escape the effects; if you were a country that relied on tourism, your market disappeared overnight, and if you were a country that relied on exporting natural resources, your buyers had almost shut shop. These two end-points describe the vast majority of African nations. As we shall see in Chapter 3, major political forces, such as China, had already taken action against the virus, irrespective of the effect it had on pivotal trading relationships, such as that maintained with the African continent. Only a handful of countries escaped economic disaster; the North and the South suffered the most, with South Africa, Namibia, and Botswana's economies contracting by 7%–8%, whilst Tunisia and Morocco suffered similar contractions. The losses were worse for tourism-dependent countries such as Cape Verde, Mauritius, and Seychelles, with their economies contracting by 10%–15%. Only Egypt and Ethiopia suffered minor contractions, although that picture has now changed after the political and militaristic strife in Ethiopia.[33]

At the beginning of this section, I wrote that there must be convergence between the social impacts of the pandemic and the economic, and it is at this point we can see that clearly. The social make-up of many African countries now came to the fore and exacerbated the pandemic, which in turn exacerbated the economic impact. For example, the understanding that the African workforce is made up of a lot of 'informal workers' has direct consequences for the spreading of the virus, as the UN note:

> Africa's significant informal sector workers (85.8 per cent of the workforce) cannot comply with social distancing and stay-at-home orders without severe consequences for their lives and livelihoods. Many household earners would be forced to choose between the virus and putting food on the table. Additionally, almost 90% of women employed in Africa work in the informal sector, with no social protections. Female headed households are particularly at risk.[34]

However, after the initial shock of 'lockdowns', skyrocketing global case rates, and a global scramble for vaccines, economic activity in the continent rebounded. Commodity prices rebounded at the end of 2020 and solidified in 2021, bringing a modicum of economic relief to those nations that rely on exporting natural resources. The sales of Eurobonds recommenced in late 2020 and increased further in 2021.[35] However, the European Investment Bank confirms that 'although private external finance flows are recovering after a sharp fall in 2020 and the international community is providing debt relief and other financial support, this will not be enough to cover all needs'.[36] Gern et al. continue by saying that although there have been signs of recovery, the reality is that 'the pandemic is likely to have long-term implications for development due to effects on human and physical capital formation'.[37] As Sanchez-Pararmo et al. succinctly state: 'the impact of the COVID-19 pandemic is largest for the world's poorest'.[38]

Estimates regarding what the continent needs to 'recover' vary from $285 billion just to respond to the pandemic and over $500 billion to 'get back on track'.[39] Others have predicted that a 'sustainable and inclusive' recovery that seeks to incorporate meeting key global goals (such as the SDGs or particular climate aims) may require up to an additional $1 trillion of investment annually.[40] What is abundantly clear, however, is that if the continent is going to experience a sustainable and inclusive recovery, it will be very gradual indeed.

2.4 Conclusion

If the African continent is to recover in a sustainable and inclusive manner, the reality is that it will need help doing so. Hopefully, at this point of the book, my underlying sentiment is being revealed. This 'help' should not be charity but collaborative. The absence of real long-term assistance after the colonial era, which was exacerbated time and time again with economic/neoliberal debt treatment initiatives, is still having consequences. A large number of African nations responded well to the MDRI and utilised the fiscal space well to incorporate key and progressive policies that were attached to the initiative, but their fundamentals were still very weak. Although the pandemic hit the continent at the very worst time (in relation to its post-colonial development), the gains made are not lost forever. However, it needs help.

That help may take many forms, and this book's suggestions are obviously not the only ones that have been put forward. The continent can be developed in a variety of ways, and if we look at its progression, it was on track to do so. However, now help is needed, and one way in which that help can be delivered is by allowing the countries to work through their debt problems. Needing to divert resources to the health of a country so that it can survive the pandemic and get back on its economic feet is not an inappropriate need. However, the available resources are being driven towards private investors. Lest we forget, every single stage of debt treatment has mainly focused on official and multilateral creditors, with private institutions only being considered in the early stages when banks were the main private holders of sovereign debt. This dynamic means that bringing creditors together was easier, and it was easier to induce them into negotiating the debt packages with the countries. However, with the entrance of private investors from the capital markets now dominating the debt picture, that picture has changed dramatically. No longer is it easy to corral all of the investors into one conversation, and nobody can induce private investors to do anything they do not want to. However, the biggest issue by a long way is the entrance of the credit rating agencies. The credit rating agencies, who theoretically act in the private investors' interests, are the gatekeeper for private investors and what they can and cannot invest in. Now, in the era of the credit rating agency, the word 'default' alone can turn every investor away, and the countries are well aware of the power the credit rating agencies have in the new dynamic. This is why if the sovereigns are to receive the help they need, one place to start is with the credit rating agencies. Can the credit rating agencies become part of the solution rather than part of the problem?

Notes

1 United Nations, 'Policy Brief: Impact of COVID-19 in Africa' (2020) *United Nations* (May) https://unsdg.un.org/sites/default/files/2020-05/Policy-brief-Impact-of-COVID-19-in-Africa.pdf 2.

2 Klaus-Jurgen Gern, Ole Luck, and Saskia Meuchelbock, 'COVID-19 in Africa and its Impact on the Economy' (2021) 158 *KIEL Policy Brief* (Sept) www.ifw-kiel.de/fileadmin/Dateiverwaltung/IfW-Publications/-ifw/Kiel_Policy_Brief/2021/KPB_158.pdf 9.

3 Osei B. Frimpong, Rigobert M. Bihuzo, and Richmond Commodore, 'The COVID-19 Pandemic in Africa: Impact, Responses, and Lessons from Ghana, the Democratic Republic of the Congo, and Rwanda' (2020) *The Wilson Center* (Sept) www.wilsoncenter.org/sites/default/files/media/uploads/documents/The%20COVID-19%20Pandemic%20in%20Africa%20-%20Impact%20Responses%20and%20Lessons.pdf 2.

4 Ibid.
5 Ibid.
6 Grace Gondwe, 'Assessing the Impact of COVID-19 on Africa's Economic Development' (2020) *United Nations Conference in Trade and Development* (July) https://unctad.org/system/files/official-document/aldcmisc2020d3_en.pdf 5.
7 Linda Nordling, 'The Pandemic Appears to Have Spared Africa So Far. Scientists Are Struggling to Explain Why' (2020) *Science* (Aug 11) www.science.org/content/article/pandemic-appears-have-spared-africa-so-far-scientists-are-struggling-explain-why.
8 The Lancet, 'Editorial' (2020) 395 *The Lancet* (May 30) www.thelancet.com/pdfs/journals/lancet/PIIS0140-6736(20)31237-X.pdf.
9 WHO, 'Rising Mortality as Africa Marks One Year of COVID-19' (2021) *WHO* (Feb 11) www.afro.who.int/news/rising-mortality-africa-marks-one-year-covid-19.
10 Hereward Holland, 'Africa's COVID-19 Third Wave Stabilises as Vaccine Levels Rise – WHO' (2021) *Reuters* (Aug 26) www.reuters.com/business/healthcare-pharmaceuticals/africas-covid-19-third-wave-stabilises-vaccine-levels-rise-who-2021-08-26/.
11 Emma Frage and Michael Shields, 'Vaccine has Entered Stage of "Vaccine Apartheid" – WHO Head' (2021) *Reuters* (May 17) www.reuters.com/business/healthcare-pharmaceuticals/world-has-entered-stage-vaccine-apartheid-who-head-2021-05-17/.
12 Alexis Arieff, Lauren Blanchard, Nicholas Cook, and Tomas Husted, 'Coronavirus Disease 2019 (COVID-19): Impact in Africa – Updated Dec 2021' (2021) *CRS* (Dec 22) https://sgp.fas.org/crs/row/IF11532.pdf.
13 BMJ, '"Vastly Underestimated" Warn Researchers' (2021) *BMJ* (Feb 17) www.bmj.com/company/newsroom/impact-of-covid-19-in-africa-vastly-underestimated-warn-researchers/.
14 Johanna Maula, 'Impact of COVID-19 on Gender Equality and Women's Empowerment in East and Southern Africa' (2021) *UN Women East and Southern Africa Regional Office* (Mar) https://reliefweb.int/sites/reliefweb.int/files/resources/abridged_-_impact_of_covid-19_on_gender_equality_and_women_empowerment_in_east_and_southern_africa.pdf IX.
15 Sam Mednick, 'Africa Detecting Just 1 in 7 Covid-19 Cases, Says WHO Study' (2021) *AP* (Oct 14).
16 Sarah Wild, 'Hidden Toll of Covid in Africa Threatens Global Pandemic Progress' (2021) *Scientific American* (Mar 25).
17 Aniefiok Udoakang, Mary Oboh, Agatha Henry-Ajala, Claudia Anyigba, Semeeh Omoleke, Alfred Amambua-Ngwa, Lily Paemka, Gordon Awandare, and Peter Quashie, 'Low COVID-19 Impact in Africa: The Multifactorial Nexus' (2021) 4 *AAS Open Research* 47.
18 Gern et al. (n 2) 5.
19 Wild (n 16).
20 Arieff et al. (12).
21 WHO (n 9).
22 UN (n 1).
23 Arieff et al. (n 12).
24 Maula (n 14).
25 Edward K. Ameyaw, Bright O. Ahinkorah, Abdul-Aziz Seidu, and Caroline Njue, 'Impact of COVID-19 on Maternal Healthcare in Africa and the Way Forward' (2021) 79 *Archives of Public Health* 223.
26 Leo Holtz, 'Covid-19's Impact on Overall Health Care Services in Africa' (2021) Brookings (Oct 12) www.brookings.edu/blog/africa-in-focus/2021/10/12/covid-19s-impact-on-overall-health-care-services-in-africa/.
27 Frimpong et al. (n 3).
28 Antonio Guterres, 'Opening Remarks at Secretary-General's End-of-year Press Encounter' (2021) *United Nations* (Dec 16) www.un.org/sg/en/node/261243.

29 Billy Agwanda, Gershon Dagba, Prince Opoku, Mark O. Amankwa, and Israel N. Nyadera, 'Sub-Saharan African and the COVID-19 Pandemic: Reflecting on Challenges and Recovery Opportunities' (2021) 37 *Journal of Developing Societies* 4 502–524.
30 UN (n 1) 5.
31 Agwanda et al. (n 29).
32 UN (n 1) 5.
33 Gern et al. (n 2) 9.
34 UN (n 1) 14.
35 Gern et al. (n 2) 12.
36 European Investment Bank, *Finance in Africa: For Green, Smart and Inclusive Private Sector Development* (2021) www.eib.org/attachments/publications/economic_report_finance_in_africa_2021_en.pdf 3.
37 Gern et al. (n 2) 12.
38 Carolina Sanchez-Pararmo, Ruth Hill, Daniel Gerszon Mahler, Ambar Narayan, and Nishant Yonzan, 'Covid-19 Leaves a Legacy of Rising Poverty and Widening Inequality' (2021) *World Bank Blog* (Oct 7).
39 ONE, *The 5 Biggest Barriers to Ending the Covid-19 Pandemic for Good* (2021) https://cdn.one.org/international/media/international/2021/10/27070252/G20-policy-platform_EN_final.pdf?akid=131280.10459304.TLCJuB&rd=1&t=31&utm_campaign=covid19&utm_medium=email&utm_source=email.
40 European Investment Bank (n 36) 3.

3 The DSSI, the Common Framework, and the Credit Rating Impasse

3.1 Introduction

Whilst the rate of growth on the African continent was slow but certainly steady before the pandemic's effects hit, the rate of decline afterwards was nothing of the sort. The rapid weakening of the health of the continent was eventually aligned to the reduced financial capacity to deal with the pandemic, and the G20 sought to act. In this chapter, we will see what action was deemed appropriate and analyse the different mechanisms put into place to help alleviate the pressure on the continent. Bearing in mind all that we know about the development of debt treatment on the continent and the rates of success from differing models, the decisions taken by the G20 and the multilateral institutions will be able to tell us all we need to know about the commitment from the global elite towards the development of the African continent. After all, the MDRI did seem to have a positive impact; thus, perhaps the decision-makers learned a valuable lesson from that approach?

What was needed was a particularly innovative approach because, in contrast to the other debt treatment initiatives developed, the environment had changed dramatically: the inclusion of private creditors who were not banks, as before, changed the dynamics completely. The world of private investment from the capital markets brings with it particular challenges. Whilst it is much easier to obtain financing from the capital markets, and that risk is then diversified, making it a much safer economic option (for the system), the challenges are substantial. We shall discuss these challenges in much greater detail in this chapter, but what is clear is that the G20, the multilateral institutions, and the people they listened to when pushing for *something*, perhaps *anything* to be done simply did not consider the challenges we will look at. The result was inevitable: abstract failure. Nearly two years into the COVID-19 pandemic, the two initiatives developed lay in tatters, and the countries they were meant to help remain in tangible economic danger, with the consequence of this being that whilst the developed world begins to hold real hope that the pandemic is soon to pass, the reality of the global scene is much different because poorer countries simply cannot fight the pandemic. The fragility of the *global* fight against the virus is far too often underplayed.

DOI: 10.4324/9781003261223-4

Once we look closer at the two initiatives developed, we will look at the reason for this book, which is to propose to you the concept of a 'credit rating impasse'. There are both deep-rooted and technical reasons for the failure of the two initiatives, and we are already on our way to understanding them in this book. However, one must be cautious in looking to attribute blame, even though it will be necessary to do so. Coulibaly et al. tell us that 'the DSSI was a well-intentioned initiative, as debt service payments had already been rising significantly for African countries due to both rising debt levels and higher shares of costlier private sector debt'.[1] Therefore, proposing to install a 'standstill' on the payments of those debts seems like, to the naked eye at least, a plausible idea that could be quickly implemented. It is for this reason that we cannot 'blame' the idea and the institutions that developed it, but the question is can these globally elite institutions not do better than develop initiatives that were *bound* to fail because of their constitution and a lack of awareness of the *consequences* that such initiatives would create? If not, then are they fit for purpose on the global stage? Perhaps not. To fail at this level means lives have been and will continue to be lost, which is unacceptable.

There are certain 'pillars' to the dynamic this book is focusing on, and they will be assessed in turn. The multilateral institutions and G20 will be assessed via the assessment of the initiatives they developed, but there will be a laser-like focus on the investors themselves. Private creditors, as relatively new entrants to the dynamic, need much more analysis than they have currently received. Whilst it will take much more than this book to do that, their mere presence in the sovereign debt dynamic could be the study of a whole field in itself. We will see elements of self-interest, manipulation, informational campaigns akin to propaganda, and systemic protection that sits above all else in an ideological manner. Then, we have the credit rating agencies.

Readers of my work will know that I am no cheerleader for the credit rating agencies. Their performance and conduct over the years have been nothing short of scandalous, and the concept of scandal has been applied here to them as well; however, not by me. In this instance, we shall see how the *structure* of the concept of *private business* plays out and affects everything around it. Whilst in the past, credit rating agencies have been guilty of profiteering and colluding *against* investors, in this instance, they are fulfilling a systemic duty that makes it difficult for them to do anything else. We will assess that systemic duty in more detail, but the implications are impactful. If this is not a case of the 'naughty' credit rating agencies transgressing again, then what should be done with them? They cannot be punished if they are not transgressing, but perhaps it is just a case that they are not *helping*. What if it is not their role to help in this instance? I will present the case that there is a capacity to allow the credit rating agencies to be more facilitative of the wider goals in hand relating to sovereign debt and particularly vulnerable sovereign debt, but that other 'pillars' need to take certain action to allow the rating agencies to do just that. Then, of course, they would need to be incentivised purely because of the ideology of private business, but it is certainly not impossible. In the next chapter, we will discuss this 'plan' to allow rating agencies to be more facilitative, and in the following chapter, we will propose a legal framework to bring certain actions to pass, but first, we must understand why the pandemic-related debt treatment initiatives have not worked so far.

3.2 The Debt Service Suspension Initiative 2020

The DSSI sought to resolve a particular problem, and that problem needs to be contextualised. The world's most vulnerable countries were classified as being eligible for the initiative, and for the 70+ countries identified, their recent history reveals an alarming pattern. The fiscal space provided to said countries through recent rounds of debt treatment allowed those countries to borrow from the private markets at a rapid rate, and the World Bank suggests that this was abundantly clear within the data on country lending rates. For example, whilst many low- and middle-income countries borrowed from the capital markets,

> the external debt stock of DSSI-eligible countries accumulated at nearly twice the rate of that in other low- and middle-income countries in 2019. The combined external debt stock of DSSI-eligible countries rose 9 percent in 2019 to $744 billion, equivalent on average to 33 percent of their combined GNI (measured in nominal terms).[2]

This rapid rise in borrowing, at a time when the capital markets were more open than ever to sovereign debtors, created a perfect storm. In the space of nearly ten years, DSSI-eligible countries had aggregately doubled their borrowing. Whilst the official creditors (both bilateral and multilateral) still owned the slight majority of the DSSI-eligible debt outstanding, the private sector's share was and is rapidly increasing. At the end of 2019, the World Bank says that obligations to private investors totalled just over $100 billion, which is five times more than in 2010. This brought the private market's total of the DSSI-eligible debt held to 19%, up from 8% in 2010.[3] However, even when we say 'private creditors', it is important to acknowledge the variance within that category:

> Obligations to private creditors are owed mostly to bondholders. Public and publicly guaranteed debt owed to private creditors totalled $102 billion at end-2019, equivalent to 16 percent of DSSI-eligible countries' combined long-term external public debt stock. Most of this debt, 65 percent, was owed to bondholders, with the remaining 35 percent of obligations owed to commercial banks and other private entities, including commodity trading companies. Governments have used funds raised from bond issues for budgetary support, infrastructure projects, and refinancing of prior bond issues to take advantage of longer maturities and lower interest rates. Debt owed to other private creditors includes company and commercial bank

> loans with official support (guarantees) from bilateral export credit agencies or multilateral institutions. Most of this debt has been used to finance large-scale infrastructure projects, with some collateralized against future export receipts for oil or other commodities.

Furthermore, there is a clear concentration with regards to the countries utilising the capital markets:

> Obligations to private creditors were concentrated in a few countries. Eighteen DSSI-eligible countries accounted for 90 percent of debt owed to all private creditors by DSSI countries at end 2019, and 92 percent of that was owed to bondholders. In these 18 countries, private creditors' share in end-2019 public and publicly guaranteed debt stock averaged 33 percent and ranged from 60 percent in Côte d'Ivoire to 13 percent in Pakistan, the largest debtor among DSSI countries. Except for Cabo Verde and Chad, all DSSI- eligible countries with a significant share of debt owed to private creditors have issued eurobonds and half of the 18 countries are blend IBRD/IDA or IBRD borrowers assessed as creditworthy for market-based financing.[4]

This concentration, when analysed country to country, is concerning. For example, in Zambia, recent issues between the country and its private creditors have revealed an indebtedness that is simply not sustainable. The influx of private credit, when combined with the country's debt-based relationship with China, means that its debt pile stands at 78% of its GDP, with Zambia spending more than two-thirds of its annual tax revenue on servicing loans. This figure was reported in 2020 and has grown since. In contrast, the country can only afford to spend 9.1% of its budget on public healthcare.[5] Thus, whilst the debt issue is widespread, there is also the problem of acute pressure within particular economies that has the potential to be ruinous to the citizens within those jurisdictions. It was on that basis that the G20 called for something to be done to alleviate that building pressure, and the DSSI was their first attempt.

On 15th April 2020, the G20 issued a communique within which the agreement to develop the DSSI was detailed. The initiative would provide for a suspension of principal and interest payments on debts due specifically between 1st May and 31st December 2020. This would apply to the debt held by bilateral creditors only (more on the multilateral institutions and private creditors shortly). In terms of who the DSSI would apply to, those classified by the UN as 'least developed countries' would be able to apply to enter, as too would the 'IDA-countries', which were the countries deemed eligible to borrow from the World Bank's 'International Development Association'.[6] As with every debt treatment initiative, there were eligibility procedures over and above being classified as eligible. First, a country must take the proactive step of making a formal request to their bilateral creditors. Second, the country must already be receiving some sort of IMF-based financial assistance, or at least it must have made a formal request to do so. Third, the country must formally commit to using the created fiscal space to benefit its citizens in a particular manner, but it must be in relation to the pandemic crisis, that is, increased healthcare spending or economic policy development to the same end. Fourth, the country must not contract any new non-concessional borrowing, meaning that there could be no new private debt incurred during the period of debt service suspension (there could be occasions where non-concessional borrowing was allowed, but only with the expressed permission of the IMF).[7]

This is, as we know well enough by now, standard procedure. The requirement to be genuinely vulnerable, financially speaking, and pairing it with what is, in effect, structural adjustment, is the international approach to debt treatment. The focus on bilateral debt meant that it made more sense for some countries to participate than others, although there were benefits to be gained for most. Four countries were immediately ruled out of being eligible because of their ongoing arrears with either or both the IMF and the World Bank (Eritrea, Sudan, Syria, and Zimbabwe), but eventually, 73 countries were identified as being potentially eligible. Of the 73, 46 came forward very early to declare their participation in the initiative, with the majority coming from sub-Saharan Africa. Of the countries that did not confirm their participation in the scheme, 11 of them were already in severe debt distress and essentially needed different help than the DSSI would have afforded.

The concept of debt service suspension needs to be understood, and even more so through the lens with which we are analysing this 'story' in this book. Clearly, debt service *suspension* means that the payments are suspended and moved further down the road, not cancelled. Under the DSSI, the countries would get three years to pay off what they suspended, with a one-year grace period. However, tellingly, the G20 and the multilateral institutions administering the initiative were at pain to ensure it was clear that

> the suspension of debt payments will be carried out in a way that ensures that deferred payments will be adjusted to ensure that creditors will face no losses on the value of the delayed payments, this is referred to as net present value neutral or NPV-neutral.

As the Eurodad report neatly explains, 'the upshot is that this costs creditors nothing, and borrowing countries will simply have larger repayments to make once the suspension period ends'.[8] The only way this makes sense is if the approach was designed to encourage as many bilateral creditors to participate in the initiative. We must remember that those bilateral creditors were also facing the pandemic and having to deal with unique financial pressures. However, whilst it may have made sense in terms of generating participation from bilateral creditors, in a myriad of other ways, the initiative was flawed before it had even started.

3.2.1 Structural Issues With the DSSI

Forcing debtors to pay their delayed payments after three years, with a grace period of a year, was not the problem. However, forcing debtors to pay their delayed payments after three years in an NPV-neutral manner so that creditors face no costs creates a problem. In the previous chapter, we saw how the pandemic had particularly acute effects on the world's most vulnerable countries, often even before the first case of the virus had been detected on the shores of the vulnerable countries. This came after a period of slow growth, all of which was based on very weak fundamentals for a number of very different reasons (as we know). Let us park that understanding to the side for one brief moment and consider something else:

> It is worth noting that deferred official debt payments under the DSSI are expected to be repaid in full between 2022 and 2024, when participating countries already have huge repayment obligations falling due. According to Eurodad calculations based on the data provided by the World Bank, the 68 beneficiary countries for which data is available, have around $115 billion scheduled to be repaid in public external debt in 2022, 2023 and 2024. The 46 countries that have requested participation in the DSSI will be required between 2022 and 2024 to pay back not only the $5.3 billion of postponed payments, but also the $71.54 billion of pre-existing commitments, plus any other debt contracted after 2018.[9]

Now let us add to this the picture of vulnerable countries slowly regaining their footing after decades of financial upheaval – all after centuries of colonialism – and the picture looks complete; can this be defined as 'help'? It could also be interpreted as the reestablishment of debt dependency. The sentiment, essentially, is that whilst the world will be attempting to build itself up again after the global pandemic in 2022, 2023, and 2024, the world's most vulnerable countries will be left to fend for themselves and maintain the flow of funding irrespective. The idea that the world's most vulnerable can attempt to meet targets like those contained in the SDGs and the array of climate accords under such conditions is nothing short of lunacy.

The problems with the DSSI are all interlinked; thus, it is difficult to know where to start. For example, S&P discusses in an early report on the DSSI that the real question being played out by debtor countries was whether to apply, or not. The reason for this, according to S&P, was that simple cost-benefit considerations were taking place within the countries and the answers were not always as clear as the G20 would have initially imagined. Before we get to perhaps the biggest issue, the core structure of having to repay the monies deferred for up to four years was clearly of concern for participating countries, so much so that the DSSI's repayment limits were extended to six years to compensate.[10] However, worries remained and the slow take-up of the DSSI simply compounded matters. S&P also suggest that the ban on any further non-concessional borrowing is a further impediment for numerous countries who see benefit in seeking finances from the capital markets.[11] There may be many reasons why a country would prefer to contract with the capital markets rather than seek bilateral debt, or from elsewhere, such as flexibility, prestige, building better access, and less stringent terms. Removing this possibility from vulnerable countries in return for postponed relief from bilateral debt only is short-sighted, and the reduced uptake points to this reality. It was not surprising then that the G20 eased this restriction not long after establishing the DSSI, but the reputational damage of the initiative was already done – sovereigns with ratings that were not hovering around default status were going out of their way to make it abundantly clear to the marketplace that they did not want to join the DSSI.[12]

The largest issue, however, is that of the private creditors and their relationship with the dynamic. Before we look at that relationship and the issues that come from it in more detail, a much larger consideration is worth mentioning: perspective. Whilst developing a plan quickly in response to a crisis and then altering it slightly based on the feedback one receives is an acceptable practice, it appears the DSSI was so off the mark initially that serious questions need to be raised. It is difficult to understand how the process of suspending payments for three years when the data was clear that this would just push the problem further down the road whilst offering very little liquidity for the countries at hand and ultimately putting the countries into an untenable position in a few years' time came to be the prominent position taken by the G20 and the multilateral institutions. When we consider next that the relationship between the private creditors, sovereigns, and credit rating agencies was completely misunderstood, we need to question whether this was merely incompetence or something far worse. The effects of whatever we may deem it as have been particularly damaging already as the world's most vulnerable continue to fight against the pandemic with both hands tied behind their backs.

Once the initiative was up and running, it quickly became clear that the DSSI was 'too shallow to meet the fiscal needs of the inequality pandemic around us', as said by the Chief of the World Bank, David Malpass.[13] It was also noted that because of the lack of depth of the DSSI, finance ministers were essentially being forced to face 'impossible decisions' because whilst the developed world printed more money and flooded their economy with it, developing nations were forced to play by the old rules, which has been referred to as a classic example of the international 'double standard'.[14] One of the main reasons why the DSSI's reach was so shallow was because its impact is only as strong as the will of those that participate, and that list is very short indeed. Incredibly, private creditors and multilateral institutions are not part of the DSSI. Moreover, leading bilateral creditors such as China, India, and countries in the Middle East are not part of the DSSI. It is no wonder then that aims for $12 billion's worth of fiscal space that was predicted came in at just over $5 billion.

We will look at the private creditors and bilateral creditors (outside of the Paris Club), but for the multilateral institutions, surely, they would be part of an international campaign to reduce the debt burden on vulnerable countries? Multilateral debt is one of the largest sectors of debt affecting the vulnerable countries identified for the DSSI. Research suggests that the DSSI-eligible countries will be sending over $9 billion to multinational development banks and the World Bank during the May–December initial freezing period, with the World Bank expecting $2 billion of that total. However, they will not be implementing any DSSI-related assistance and will be expecting every cent of that $2 billion. This is purely on the basis that the World Bank does not want its pristine AAA credit rating affected. Its rationale is that a reduction in its credit rating will reduce its ability to lend to countries in crisis, as will a reduction in the monies it expects to receive. This has the added effect of breeding inequality between the creditors, with one sector (say, private commercial creditors) then thinking that why should they forego their payments as they will just be funnelled into paying the World Bank and other creditors? This is the psychology underlying the general impasse being witnessed in the sovereign debt sector.

Yet, it has been the arrival of the private credit sector that is causing the most problems from a debt treatment perspective. It reminds one of the Longfellow poem (There was a little girl) in that 'when she was good, she was very good indeed, but when she was bad, she was horrid';[15] in this instance, the influx of flexible finance was very good indeed for the vulnerable countries as they tried their best to grow sustainably, but when it all went wrong and the flexible financing became inflexible, it was and is certainly horrid. Recounting the story of how the DSSI initially developed tells us, at once, the naiveite of those tasked with designing the initiative and the unwarranted but unwavering belief in the marketplace.

As the G20 announced their plans for the initiative in April 2020, the Institute for International Finance (IIF) had already started its back-channel negotiations with the leading figures within the G20.[16] The IIF was created in the early 1980s by a collection of nearly 40 banks as a response to the debt crises of the era. Its mission is to be 'the most influential global association of financial institutions' and it has more than 450 members.[17] In this role as a leading influencer, the IIF wrote a letter to the heads of the IMF, World Bank, Paris Club, and G20 finance ministers detailing their 'grave concern to debt sustainability posed by the COVID-19 pandemic'. In that letter, the IIF put forward the idea that all creditors, including private creditors, should 'forbear payment default' until the end of the year (2020), essentially supporting the idea of the DSSI'.[18] The G20 communique detailing the initiative then officially called upon the private creditors, 'working through the Institute of International Finance, to participate in the initiative on comparable terms'.[19] In that instance, the G20 had made two serious mistakes.

The first mistake was to focus on the IIF as the vehicle for private creditors. As Stichele explains, 'through its longstanding contacts with the G20, the IIF was designated as the coordinator for the private sector, although many private sector creditors to DSSI countries were not members of the IIF'.[20] This favouring of an institute that did not contain all of the necessary members was problematic. However, the second mistake was to leave too much room for manoeuvre for the IIF. It is questionable whether the governments of the G20 could even compel private endeavours to forego any payments due, but the G20 was quick to support the notion of private business and the freedom that it needs. Initial calls for 'comparable treatment' and participation were full of optimism, buoyed by the early soundings from the IIF. Yet, just weeks later, the IIF would produce another letter, and the tone had changed this time. This time, the IIF spelt out all of the hurdles to private sector involvement and was at pains to make clear that any participation needed to be conducted on a *voluntary* basis. The G20 quickly and audibly agreed, with the Saudi Chair of the G20 finance track publicly commenting that governments 'should avoid imposing anything on the private investors as it may distort markets and limit future demand for emerging market debt from the private sector'.[21]

In addition, but now with underlying G20 backing, the IIF began an informational campaign to protect the position of its members. As the IIF and its members began quickly to understand that there was at least some potential for a wave of defaults, the campaign went into overdrive and began with the IIF writing, on 1st May, that there was a 'complex landscape' to be reviewed, and within which there were many key legal and practical hurdles. The first of which was that any participation would have to be on a voluntary basis, and that each private creditor would need to make its own assessment on what exactly constituted 'NPV neutrality'. Second, each private creditor would need to undertake assessments to understand whether being involved in such a debt treatment initiative was even legal, owing to the 'fiduciary duties' that the principals (managers) of the investors owed to their agents (base investors). We will return to this relationship between the two end-points shortly. Then, each application for debt treatment would have to be done individually; to that end, the IIF produced its 'Terms of Reference for Voluntary Private Sector Participation in the G20/Paris Club Debt Service Suspension Initiative'.[22] Whether this was helpful is another story entirely, although the IIF appeared to be pleased with its effect: '[the ToR is] the best possible response at this time to the call from the official sector for private sector participation'.[23]

The reality is that the IIF ToR may have represented 'the best possible response', but what is also true is that this is very telling indeed. The IIF knew full well that debtor countries could not have made use of the ToR because of the credit rating impasse – with one of the reasons being that the leading credit rating agencies are themselves members of the IIF – but also because the ToR apparently allowing for requests of private creditors was part of a much larger campaign to scare debtors off from doing exactly what the ToR allowed to. Because the IIF and its members were 'concerned that the Debt Service Suspension Initiative will trigger a wave of sovereign downgrades, defaults and cross-defaults' the approach was taken to warn of fiduciary duties causing problems for private creditors, and also that it was "imperative" that borrowing countries "be well-informed" about the potential consequences for market access when requesting debt service suspension (especially from the private sector)'.[24] Not only have the potential consequences of engaging been played down since by leading commentators,[25] but also in the cases where a country has requested debt treatment from its private creditors, the consequences have certainly not been as severe as the IIF initially warned.[26] The reasoning for the IIF taking this approach needs to be investigated in depth because it has been allowed to pass without scrutiny; given the self-appointed and then officially backed centrality of the institute, it is simply not acceptable. With regards to the conduct of the IIF, Bolton et al. spelt everything out for us succinctly:

> Taken as a whole, the IIF's 1 May letter sent three messages to the official sector and to the sovereign debtor community generally. First, rather than decline to participate in the DSSI, the commercial creditors would prefer not to be *asked* to participate. This explains the repeated alarms about credit rating downgrades, loss of market access and the imperative need for the debtor countries to be 'well-informed' about the dire consequences of even asking the private sector for a suspension of debt service payments.
>
> Second, if a debtor country does *ask* for a suspension of private sector debt service, it must understand that this is likely to be a lengthy creditor-by-creditor, perhaps instrument-by-instrument, process. In addition, the resulting deferment of debt service payments may be more expensive than the 'NPV neutral' suspension of bilateral payments. The implication here is that by the time a debt service suspension for a private creditor is negotiated, documented and executed, there may be very little of 2020 left in which the suspension will operate. A debtor country may thus suffer all of the negative consequences of having asked for a deferment of commercial debt service payments without in fact ever deferring many (or any) such payments.
>
> Third, the IIF 1 May letter is not a guide for how to implement a standstill on commercial debt payments. It is rather a checklist of the potential reasons that individual commercial creditors may cite as a justification for their refusal to accept such a standstill. Among these are fiduciary duties to investors, contractual commitments, regulatory requirements and national laws, 'among other considerations.'[27]

In a purely detached manner, it makes sense for the IIF to attempt to scare off requests for debt treatment because it preserves the position of *its* members. The competition that exists amongst creditors, both private and official, is intense because there is now only a particular amount of money being streamed from vulnerable countries to their array of creditors, and at some point, it is bound to run out if the situation continues as it is. What we are witnessing is jostling for position before that point occurs, and nobody is innocent. There will be many who will argue that this is how the creditor/debtor relationship has to be and that the debtor should not have contracted for the finances if it could not repay them. However, this is not a company the creditors are dealing with, but an overly indebted vulnerable country that is consistently having to divert its resources from its citizens or, to put it another way, *human beings*. Nevertheless, the campaign of pressure and fear has been relentless. Leading market participants have been openly questioning why any country would want to threaten their market access,[28] whilst others have been declaring 'the sanctity of contracts'.[29]

Referencing the 'IIF' has the effect, unfortunately, of masking certain truths within the private credit sector. Some of the world's largest investors are members, and their relationship with the debt we are focusing on is important to put into context. For example, although the interest rates on the debt are considered to be the 'insurance' against the level of risk posed by the debtor, investors will ensure that their position is protected from loss, often many times over. Investors will purchase insurance on that debt; however, in addition, 'many creditors normally hedge their debt exposure to protect themselves against payment default – "through derivatives, sub-participations, insurance, repackaging, or other means"'.[30] Another example Stichele cites is the case of BlackRock, a major institutional investor. It has been suggested that BlackRock owns about $16 billion in middle- and low-income debt, which equates to about 0.2% of its assets under management; in 2020, it returned nearly $4 billion to its shareholders after making a record profit. The insinuation here is that the leading private investors have plenty of leeway to consider negotiating their debt holdings with the sovereign states; they just choose not to.

It is not surprising then that the moral compass of the private investors has been called into question. Bolton et al. make the impassioned point that this is not a usual debtor/creditor relationship and should not be treated as such:

> In normal times, commercial actors may be expected to behave like commercial actors. There are other times, however, when venality should be tempered by a sense of social responsibility. A pandemic that shuts down much of the world's economy is such a circumstance. Forcing governments in the middle of this pandemic to choose between their credit reputations and the lives of their citizens is, we believe, self-evidently wrong. The DSSI does not ask creditors to forgive debt service payments falling due during the balance of this year, only defer those amounts (with interest) to allow limited financial resources to be devoted to crisis amelioration. It therefore seeks restraint, not charity.[31]

The simplicity of what is being asked of the private creditors, when viewed in comparison with the way in which the private creditors have responded, may mean one of two things. First, it could mean that the private creditors are simply venal entities and do not accept nor care about the human damage that this impasse is causing. This is entirely possible. However, in a world where the public, especially the Western public, is becoming more attuned to the environmental, social, and governance effects of big business, there is a risk for institutional investors in taking this approach; many large investors essentially hold the funds of the public via pension holdings and the like, and are not keen to inflict reputational damage upon themselves (so the theory goes, and I am not too sure that I would align myself to that theory). Second, it could be the case that there are structural impediments that bind their hands.

This book is of the opinion that the latter is more likely true. Whilst it is more likely that the IIF, in promoting its own interest as an organisation, have gotten the tone very, very wrong, the underlying sentiment of structural impediments holds up under scrutiny. The largest one, as far as we are concerned in this book, is the existence of the credit rating impasse and the dynamic between sovereign debtors and private creditors. Yet, there are other structural impediments that negatively affect the ability of private creditors to participate in debt treatment initiatives, and one of the most impactful is inter-creditor dynamics.

3.2.2 The Complicated Middle Ground Between Politics and Business

To understand the structural impediments in detail, let us put ourselves in the position of a private creditor invested in sovereign debt. Let us all put aside the fair argument that when investing in low-income country debt, it is not at all certain that you will receive your investment back, as signified by the low ratings from the credit rating agencies. All that accepted, what is different to investing in a corporation, for example? For a start, the credit ratings will not be as accurate, in theory, mainly because the leading credit rating agencies have a lesser relationship with the countries in question than they do with corporates, who are often based in developed countries and have a massive incentive to work *with* the agencies. However, looking past the rating angle, one thing we would know as an investor in the corporate sector is that the only other investors will be investors like ourselves. Yes, they may be more powerful or have more influence, but we would know, roughly, their constitution and their sway over the debtor. We would also know that there will be some sort of bankruptcy procedure that provides us all, as creditors, with some sort of order should the debtor run into financial trouble. These are aspects that we can rely upon, for the most part. However, in the sovereign sector, none of that is true. We already know from our analysis of the SDRM that there is no global bankruptcy procedure for sovereigns. We also know that different types of creditors are invested in the one stream of resources being generated by the country we are invested in, and the more the sovereign gets into trouble, the more competitive it becomes in terms of fighting for our share of that ever-dwindling stream of money.

According to the World Bank, there are five main types of creditors: (1) bilateral creditors, (2) multilateral creditors, (3) suppliers' creditors, (4) commercial banks and other private entities, and (5) bonds.[32] Let us accept this list for the time being, but let us consider another concept first before continuing:

power. In the sovereign space, there are differing levels of power, and they can be very effective. The majority of the Western focus is on China and its manoeuvrings. However, before we cover the issue of the Chinese approach to sovereign debt treatment, there are other sources of influence that can be just as impactful to the position of the private creditor. For instance, we saw earlier how the World Bank 'has so far received as much in debt service payments as it is giving out in COVID-19-related grants'[33] whilst it is also the case that the proposal for the IMF to generate a pot of $500 billion in ultra-low-interest liquidity for vulnerable countries was opposed by the US, the IMF's largest shareholder.[34] With these instances in mind, the private creditors may be asking themselves why should they open themselves up to potential losses when the Western-backed international organisations are not, and what avenues of redress are there against the actions of the US and her allies. The same issues are witnessed when we consider the Chinese position.

We will assess this much more in the final chapter of the book, but we already know that Africa has been at the centre of the international 'push-and-pull' for centuries, and that is not stopping. In fact, it is evolving, and the latest player to become involved in the continent is China. Since the time of Deng Xiaoping, China has been on the fast track to modernisation and is now the world's second-largest economy. However, under the leadership of China's current president, Xi Jinping, the country is actively seeking to redress the global power balance in its favour. It is doing this in several ways, with the two most relevant for us being the 'belt-and-road' initiative and general debt-based diplomacy. The belt-and-road initiative,[35] of which a comprehensive study is far outside the bounds of this work, is essentially a coordinated project by China to join together the important parts of Asia, Eurasia, and Africa; this would forge new trading opportunities, but this also positions China as a global leader who cooperates rather than rules by coercion. Evidence of this approach can be seen across the African continent, with major infrastructure projects being completed (and more being developed) using Chinese resources and expertise. In return, the Chinese gain access to the much-needed natural resources that Africa has to offer, and which the Chinese sorely need to maintain their economic development at the historic rates it has been.

These developments have been going on for quite some time. However, it is during the COVID-19 pandemic crisis that we can see the true extent of China's commitment to the continent, even if we can never truly know the statistical bind between the two entities. For example, the World Bank reports that China, in 2019, accounted for 26% of the external debt stock of low- and middle-income countries and that in 2019 alone, their debt stock in the two categories of countries increased by 8%.[36] It has been put forward that between 2000 and 2018, China and private Chinese entities invested nearly $150 billion into large-scale African infrastructure projects, and during the last five years, more than two-thirds of that investment has gone directly into the transport and energy sectors. The same source suggests that since 2010, Chinese financial institutions have funded around 70 projects a year on the continent, with an average value of $180 million; this investment has been focused on energy and mineral-rich countries and on the east coast of the continent where China is seeking to add its belt-and-road influence.[37]

However, it is difficult to know the full picture of China's exposure to the African continent. The World Bank's Chief Economist, Carmen Reinhart, stated that the presence of China on the African continent is a 'complicating factor', continuing that 'transparency has been a sensitive issue for some time'. By this, she means that 'many loan contracts have non-disclosure agreements so they are not known about', which has the effect that 'the private sector is working on the assumption that a country's debts are lower [than they really are], and the official sector is doing its debt sustainability analysis predicated on the assumption that debts are lower'.[38]

Rogovic et al. state that there is no one standardised approach from China or its private affiliates. In describing how any past precedent can only provide us with limited insight into the future behaviour of the Chinese state or its private affiliates, the scholars confirm:

> Over the past few years, the response of Chinese policy banks to SSA sovereigns that faced liquidity pressure has not been uniform or transparent. There is evidence of some willingness of Chinese lenders to renegotiate loans, alleviating acute fiscal and balance of payments pressures. However, the lack of fulsome disclosure, consistency and predictability around the conditions attached to these restructurings mean the credit implications of Chinese policy banks' presence among a sovereign's creditors are less clear.[39]

Outside of sub-Saharan Africa, Chinese lenders have been equally as inconsistent, although Rogovic et al. do suggest that there is a consistency in one sense: 'Chinese lenders have shown a similar willingness to provide liquidity, but often in exchange for resource concessions, such as land in exchange for some debt relief'.[40]

This has led some to suggest that China is 'trapping' African countries with their debt agreements, which is something the Chinese state vehemently denies: China's Foreign Minister said recently that accusations of traps are 'simply not fact. It is speculation being played out by some with ulterior motives' and that 'this is a narrative that has been created by those who do not want to see development in Africa. If there is any trap, it is about poverty and underdevelopment'.[41] The Chinese President himself has been at the forefront of pushing for a collaborative environment between China and Africa, making it clear recently that he welcomed 'African countries aboard the express train of China's development' and that 'no one could hold back the Chinese people or the African people as we march towards rejuvenation'.[42] It can be clearly seen here that there is a much deeper narrative being developed between the two entities, and we shall see why in the last chapter of the book. However, we are attempting to consider how this relationship affects that of the private creditor;

to do that, numerous case studies have revealed the potential impact on the intra-creditor relationship within the sovereign debt sector.

Because of the credit stress across the countries China is invested in, Moody's has reported that the belt-and-road initiative will be much leaner from now on. Whilst the policy support is still of focus for the Chinese state, the development of debt relationships will be monitored and coordinated in a much more efficient manner. Nevertheless, the Chinese state and its private affiliates are becoming increasingly exposed to losses, and their strategies for dealing with this are both revealing and impactful for the position of private creditors.[43] As an aside, it is interesting to note that the majority of countries China is seeking to envelop within the belt-and-road initiative are either sub-investment grade or non-rated countries (because of the additional ideological aim to bring together the globally disenfranchised), which brings with it the need to strategise for the initiative's (and the State's) future, even if it means flexing the political muscle that China possesses. To continue, there are insightful examples in the form of Zambia and Angola that reveal to us just how China employs this strategy.

Before continuing further, two particular aspects are worth noting. First, China is not part of the Paris Club. Second, there is a constant issue between China and the West regarding how China categorises its financial institutions, that is, whether they are part of the official apparatus of the State or wholly commercial. The lack of clear differentiation in the Chinese model of capitalism causes concerns, and private creditors are often unhappy about how particular institutions are categorised and put together. For example, Zambia was an outlier in that it approached its private creditors regarding payment suspensions (Zambia was already bordering on default [and has since defaulted], meaning it had little to lose), but its request was rejected by the Eurobond holders. This was because the private creditors were concerned that any relief would simply be funnelled into Chinese banks with whom Zambia had outstanding arrears.[44] China's official lenders (e.g. policy banks) stated that they needed their arrears to be cleared before they could consider granting debt relief, although this was not enough for the Eurobond holders to be persuaded. However, it was the decision of China to redesignate some of its financial institutions that left a sour taste. For example, The Export-Import Bank of China, and the China Development Bank – both widely recognised as Chinese policy banks and non-commercial in nature – had been making non-policy loans for several years in an attempt to generate profits that could offset the 'financial drag of policy-related lending'. As such, China redesignated the China Development Bank, and any such debt relief would, therefore, be coming from a private creditor, which has a whole host of connotations as we now know. For the other private creditors, it is a clear example of an uneven playing field upon which they feel disadvantaged but have no recourse to alter the direction of events. They do, of course, have one action they can take: stay the course and not bend, and that is exactly what and why they are doing it.

Angola is another example of the intra-creditor dynamic coming under pressure. Angola is a resource-rich country, and it is no surprise that 'Angola has been the largest recipient of Chinese loans, accounting for a third of Chinese lending in Africa'.[45] The make-up of these loans is sparsely understood, with a fair share representing commodity-linked sovereign debt. Coulibaly et al. suggest that Angola has received over $10 billion in oil-backed loans, with the loans being on a non-concessionary basis and which required that 70% of the contracts go to Chinese companies.[46] However, this close connection between China and Angola (Angola is the fourth largest oil exporter to China) means that China must pay close attention to the financial health of Angola, and it has done so. Angola petitioned to join the DSSI, and it was China that had encouraged it to do so because it could potentially save $3.5 billion from doing so, with some of the savings coming against Chinese loans.[47] However, for the oil-backed loans, the renegotiations were opaque, and the precise details of how those loans were restructured are not known. China has done what it needed to protect its position. For other private creditors holding Angolan debt, the opaqueness is a major reason why they would not necessarily be inclined to open themselves up to suspensions. World Bank Chief, David Malpass, commented on this:

> For DSSI to be fully effective, there should be a standard minimum set of debt-structuring information. This will avoid the secretive rescheduling that are underway in some countries, such as Angola and Laos, often with undisclosed grace periods and terms. This fragmentation disfavors other creditors and the people in the debtor country.[48]

Again, the theme of transparency and equal footing rears its head. However, it is unlikely that China will be persuaded to do anything different, and nobody has the force to *make* them do anything differently. No doubt it is driven by business principles, but China has the addition of a cause that it has attached to its debt relationship with African countries, which has fundamentally altered the picture for everybody involved. What it does do is send a clear message to private creditors that this will never be a level playing field and hold the same rules as holding commercial debt does. That may indicate that private creditors have no choice but to be inflexible, but one could argue that there is inflexibility witnessed in every pillar of the sovereign debt sector, so why should private creditors be any different?

The position of the private creditor is of the utmost importance to us here in the book because they are, essentially, a 'new entrant' into the sovereign debt dynamic and their position needs to be understood. The modern prevalence of low- and middle-income sovereigns going to the capital markets instead of traditional lending streams means that the dynamic will not be vanishing any time soon, rather it is likely to become more entrenched. For that reason, there must be more attempts to resolve some of the underlying issues that prevent flexibility in a sector where inflexibility directly costs lives. So, what else can the private creditors do to protect themselves and allow for restructurings to take place to alleviate financial pressures on vulnerable sovereign states? One element, as we discussed earlier, would be the global development and establishment of the 'Collective Action Clause'. This chapter will move on to the position of the credit rating agencies shortly and reveal the 'credit rating impasse' in all its detail before reviewing the current debt treatment initiative developed: the Common Framework. However, before we do that, we need to continue assessing the position of the private creditor.

3.3 The Potential of the Collective Action Clause

Whilst the SDRM did not materialise, there are many market-based mechanisms that can help promote restructuring in the sovereign space. One such mechanism is the 'Collective Action Clause' (CAC). A CAC is essentially a contractual mechanism that is inserted into the contracts that govern particular bond sales and, once agreed to, serves to bound all of those signed up to the particular bond so that certain procedures can come into effect once a certain point is reached or triggered. CACs can be very helpful indeed in stopping 'holdout creditors' or major disagreements as they would have already been agreed to if and when a sovereign needs to restructure its debts. However, there are inherent elements of the CAC process which do not lend themselves well to the modern sovereign space.

The World Bank suggests that CACs can be a positive addition to the sovereign space:

> Collective action clauses are provisions of bonds that specify procedures for selecting bondholders' representatives in debt negotiations and provide for the modification of terms on bonds by a substantial majority. They generally prohibit individual bondholders from initiating litigation and require that any funds recovered through litigation be shared with all creditors. Greater use of collective action clauses could help impose majority-supported debt restructuring agreements on minority creditors, thus reducing the probability of a disorderly default.[49]

CACs are not modern developments and originated in the London bond markets in the late 1800s 'as a civilised way to organise collective decision-making when there is a plurality of creditors, ensuring also that the collective interests dominates private interests'.[50] Eventually, this private resolution would be captured within the relevant statute in the UK, but for the sovereign marketplace, there has been no option to implement such a statutory rule, as we know with failure to implement the SDRM (interestingly, Kopf tells us that the IIF were the biggest opponents of the SDRM).[51] Nevertheless, in the early 2000s, on the back of Argentina defaulting on its obligations, the IMF began to push for the worldwide implementation of CACs and achieved the desired effect.[52]

When a sovereign issues a Eurobond (a bond in a foreign denomination), it usually does so within a select number of renowned jurisdictions. Doing this allows the creditors to know that the contract they are entering into is placed within a jurisdiction that has particularly established legal systems and can, therefore, theoretically be relied upon. The major legal centres for this are London and New York (with some European hubs too). In the early 2000s, London was the host for nearly 50% of all sovereign bond issuances, mostly because the English system already had all of the necessary provisions to affect the contracts containing CACs. Empirical research found that bonds that were subject to the English law had much lower 'spreads'[53] than bonds issued in jurisdictions that did not acknowledge CACs. However, once the IMF had pushed for the global recognition of CACs, New York and the EU followed suit (in 2003),[54] and now the vast majority of sovereign bond issuances do, or at least can contain the options for CACs.[55]

Let us remember that at the time the IMF was pushing for the global implementation of CACs, it had just failed in its attempt to bring the SDRM to fruition. With the lobbying efforts of mainly the IIF, the decision was then taken to push for market-based solutions to the sovereign debt problems rather than anything formal. This may have been in the IIF and private creditors' interests, but the application of CACs in the sovereign debt space brings with it a host of issues. The issue of sovereigns being virtually unable to restructure their private debts has continued, indicating that CACs are not necessarily the answer, but this is because CACs were designed for the corporate issuance market, and not the sovereign.

One of the most impactful issues is that a CAC can only apply to a particular debt instrument. Many sovereign bond issuances contain a number of instruments, with the result being that a CAC cannot effectively reduce the possibilities of a 'disorderly restructuring'. As the World Bank explain:

> Collective action clauses may not provide sufficient protection against a disorderly restructuring. They only bind acceptance of a debt negotiation by creditors with the same instrument, so they would not help resolve disputes across instruments or classes of creditors. That is, they would not aggregate claims across creditors. Nor would they address the large portion of the existing stock of debt that not include collective action clauses. And it may be difficult to get some issuers (particularly issuers rated below investment-grade) to include such clauses in bond instruments for fear that this would signal the intention to default and erode the issuer's competitive position in the international debt markets.[56]

This lack of retroactivity also may affect sovereigns who have issued long-term bonds before CACs were a given practice in a particular jurisdiction, although this scenario will be limited in the current age.

CACs can also play an important role in changing the power dynamics within the debtor/creditor relationship. A good example is the variance within sovereign bond issuances. A sovereign bond exchange can involve 'dozens or even hundreds of instruments, and considering all of these claims on their own merit would raise transaction costs to a prohibitive level'.[57] Gelpern confirms the same:

> In fact, sovereign bond contracts are not nearly as standardised as market participants and policy makers seem to suggest. It is common to see a handful of negotiated terms embedded in a mish-mash of different generation industry models, sprinkled with bits of creative expression that no one can explain, usually attributed to some long-forgotten lawyers. At least some of the variation appears to be deliberate. However, to the extent that it is inadvertent, variation can be costly. For example, it can make contracts internally inconsistent, vulnerable to opportunistic lawsuits and errors of judicial interpretation. Variation could also make debt instruments less liquid, especially during periods of market stress.[58]

Therefore, in instances where sovereigns need to restructure their debts, the sovereigns will often offer their private creditors simplified offers to reduce unnecessary transaction costs. There have been multiple examples (Argentina and Greece, chief amongst them) where creditors have been offered a smaller array of new bonds to choose from (in the Greek case, creditors were offered only one new instrument). This, theoretically, allows for a resolution to be agreed to. However, this heavily advantages the debtor, who 'typically exploit existing information asymmetries to their favour and underestimate their solvency'.[59] This can have numerous important effects. First, issuers have been found to, sometimes, negotiate a reduction on their debt that was larger than what was warranted. This can lead to the second effect: creditor punishment. Creditors, who become aware of such practices may refuse to do business with the sovereign in future (this happened to Russia in the late 1990s), and the reputational damage can raise interest rates on future bond sales as creditors factor in the potential behavioural issues of the sovereign when entering into bond sales. Kopf argues that one element that could reduce this strain on the sovereign would be for it to pay for the bondholder committees that need to be formed to develop representation for the bondholders. In the US corporate scene, it is the debtors who pay for such committees to be formed (which may be a significant cost if a debtor has an array of creditors), but on the sovereign scene, no such practice exists. It is the creditors who would foot that bill, and that is simply another prohibitive cost to entering into restructurings.[60]

Simply put, CACs are useful but not the absolute answer. Schwarz explains how even the celebrated function of stopping holdout creditors from blocking a restructure is not absolute as creditors could potentially purchase vote-blocking positions and achieve their aims that way.[61] He argues that market-based mechanisms can only go so far and a multilateral bankruptcy framework for sovereigns is needed. Yet, as we know from the SDRM, this 'is not currently political feasible'. He puts this into the context of a more recent attempt to put something more formal into practice when Bolivia led the charge on behalf of 77 developing nations and China; predictably, the US and the EU opposed the resolution. As Schwarz confirms, 'although the United Nations Conference on Trade and Development has been tasked with moving the General Assembly's approach forward, there is scepticism as to whether any such framework is feasible without US or EU support'.[62] This is telling, especially in light of the analysis that opened the book concerning the preservation of the 'old order'.

Nevertheless, this causes us to ask a simple question: if market-based mechanisms cannot help the current situation, and there is no Western political will to establish a formal bankruptcy system, then what can move the dial? What can be done to allow struggling sovereigns to restructure their debts with private creditors? This book argues that the answer lies within the credit rating agency dynamic.

3.4 The Credit Rating Impasse

A fundamental relationship exists between the international credit rating agencies and private investors/creditors. In the corporate sector, credit rating agencies have become a centralised financial institution because, at its core, the credit rating industry exists to predict the likelihood that an investor in a bond will see their money back and according to the terms of the bond issuance. The relationship is much more complex than that, but at its core, that is what the credit rating industry does for the financial system. It is clear from this rudimentary explanation that theoretically, the investment would be massively curtailed were it not for the existence of credit rating agencies. As the world transitioned towards the capital markets as we know them and away from traditional lending practices (from banking institutions etc.), the place for the credit rating agencies was crystalised. However, how does this translate to the sovereign scene?

In reality, credit rating agencies have been, for a long time, almost useless in the sovereign sector. Official creditors would not be overly inclined to consider their ratings because their constitution is very different from private creditors, and the private creditors who would be interested in investing in sovereign bonds were large banking institutions, who likely have a better analytical framework than most credit rating agencies would have. With that in mind, it would be unlikely that any sovereign would want to pay for the credit rating on their bonds, and thus credit rating agencies traditionally would not have endeavoured to do so if there was no profit to be made. That has traditionally been the relationship between the credit rating agencies and the sovereign space (with some exceptions).

However, the entrance of the private creditors into the sovereign space brought with it the credit rating agencies, who operate almost synergistically with the interests of private capital. This is because the credit rating agencies are, to all intents and purposes, the 'gatekeepers' to the capital markets, and if countries want access to the capital markets, they must become exposed to the inner workings (and effects) of the credit rating agencies. Therefore, in this current pandemic-related crisis, the credit rating agencies have become a central pillar to the problem and (as I argue here) the potential solution. This is becoming clearer by the day and was emphasised in the opening quote to the book, taken from the UN Secretary-General (which is a rare occurrence).

Before explaining the different nuanced issues in this regard (and there are plenty), it is perhaps useful to simplify the credit rating impasse. Simply, the credit rating impasse explains the instance where a vulnerable country cannot participate in the DSSI or Common Framework, or even approach private creditors bilaterally, because of the threat from credit rating agencies that doing so would be considered a default-worthy event, and the sovereign rating would be altered to reflect that. The result of this would be that if downgraded to default, the country would not be able to renegotiate properly anyway as many bond contract clauses would be triggered by the drop in rating. It would also exclude the country from the capital markets for a particular length of time, governed by the agencies, meaning any hopes of recovery would be shot down immediately. There are several reasons why a country may not want to participate in the multilateral initiatives being set up but none bigger than the credit rating impasse.

The credit rating impasse perhaps presents itself the clearest when we consider the inner workings of many sovereign bonds. Kearse explains that defaulting on an obligation usually 'triggers' some predetermined set of actions that seek to protect the creditor. These may be ceasing to make any further advancements, demanding immediate repayment of the outstanding debt, and/or enforcing the security. In addition, there are 'cross-default' arrangements, which describe the scenario whereby a default from the debtor in another debt arrangement with other creditors can trigger particular actions in the original debt arrangement. These cross-default mechanisms act as an early warning system for creditors, but they also seek to ensure equality amongst creditors so that no one creditor is paid out of a potentially dwindling pot of resources first.[63] This is why being downgraded into default by a credit rating agency for even publicly considering joining the DSSI or Common Framework could be ruinous for the country in question.

Kearse continues by stating that 'the non-payment of debt by DSSI participating governments may result in a default/cross-default under their private creditors' loan documentation. Nonetheless, borrowers may have the option to request waivers from their creditors and/or request to restructure/refinance their debt.'[64] Whilst the IIF and its members have indeed developed a waiver that countries can utilise when approaching their private creditors (however, the waiver is complicated and only applies on a case-by-case, creditor-by-creditor basis), it is irrelevant. The reason can be found in the warnings given by the credit rating agencies when the G20 and the multilateral institutions *suggested* that debt treatment given by official creditors via the DSSI should be on *comparable* terms to the private sector; the mere suggestion of that key word *comparability* had the rating agencies warning of downgrades to default for any country even considering approaching their private creditors. For their part, the rating agencies have been crystal clear from the outset.

Fitch Ratings, for example, confirmed that its Issuer Default Ratings would 'only refer to defaults on commercial debt, participation [in the DSSI] would not constitute a default', solely because the insistence on comparable treatment between official and private debt was very quickly dropped by the G20 and the multilateral institutions.[65] Whilst all three agencies have been monitoring the situation closely, Moody's has been leading the charge to put countries on reviews for downgrades, which can be financially damaging for countries. This put Moody's on a collision course with the UN, who made the point forcefully to the agency that the DSSI would ultimately improve the countries' debt sustainability, adding that 'borrowing countries should come out of the programme with stronger credit than if they had not participated'.[66] The agency, for its part, simply repeated its line that if private creditors are ever at risk of losing their investment, then the rating needed to reflect that. Once the G20 backed down and removed the insistence on comparable dent treatment, registrations accelerated sharply because the countries in question knew the consequences if the comparable treatment mandate had been maintained. Moody's responded with the factual point that 'the IMF and the World Bank are in a very influential position, [able] to exert pressure on sovereigns to implement measures that could ultimately be credit negative for the private sector', which in effect means that any participation with the multilateral institutions via the DSSI needed to be assessed for any potential credit-negative impacts on the private sector.

This, of course, has led to the rating agencies receiving a torrent of criticism. Jayati Ghosh commented:

> If the G-20 countries are serious about improving developing countries' debt positions during the COVID-19 crisis, they should begin by supporting the temporary suspension of credit ratings. In the medium term, regulators must take action to ensure that rating agencies are fulfilling their intended market-stabilising role. Tackling conflicts of interest, such as by limiting agencies' dependence on payments from those they rate, is essential.[67]

In 2020, the UN's new Independent Expert on the Effects of Foreign Debt and other related international financial obligations of states on the full enjoyment of all human rights, particularly economic, social, and cultural rights, Yuefen Li, was tasked with reporting on the rating agency issue. In 2021, she published, via the Human Rights Council of the UN, her report entitled 'Debt Relief, Debt Crisis Prevention and Human Rights: The Role of Credit Rating Agencies'. In it, she noted that there were serious issues with the agencies, ranging from wide-ranging conflicts of interests, procyclical ratings, ratings with ideological biases attached, and a lack of accountability within the system governing the agencies. She concluded:

> The gravity of the sovereign debt situation, exacerbated by the COVID-19 pandemic, has once again proved the need to regulate and reform credit rating agencies, which should be taken as part of the reform of the international financial architecture and debt crisis prevention and resolution. In this regard, the consideration of allowing developing countries to have access to financial resources to strengthen economic, social, and cultural rights during special circumstances, including situations such as the COVID-19 pandemic and natural disasters, and to assist them in obtaining long-term economic development should be part of the credit rating assessment equation.[68]

Bolton et al. make a different but equally passionate point:

> For their part, the credit rating agencies appear to have approached the DSSI in a particularly wooden manner. Sovereign credit downgrades may well be coming. If the effect of the pandemic on export markets, commodity prices, remittance flows, tax collections and exchange rates is even half as bad as the official sector fears it might be, the credit ratings of many countries will inevitably be negatively affected. To threaten a downgrade simply because a country seeks to defer a debt service payment in the middle of a pandemic, however, is both *morally obtuse* and economically short-sighted. By redeploying those funds toward crisis amelioration the country may succeed in limiting the damage to its population and economy. This should raise, not lower, its esteem in the eyes of the credit rating agencies.[69]

That the credit rating agencies have internal (and associated external) problems is clear for all to see. The lack of an international regulator in the financial sense, at least with the influence to undertake what is being requested above, means that the requests are mostly academic regrettably. However, it is this concept raised by Bolton et al. that presents the interesting question of whether private entities such as the rating agencies have any moral responsibility. Although corporate undertakings will, in some way, affect the lives of human beings, the difference between rating corporate and sovereigns, in relation to *effect*, is stark. With these threats of downgrades to default, there is a clear effect on the futures of human beings in the countries being threatened. Resources are actively being diverted from healthcare initiatives into the servicing of mostly private debt because the rating agencies would not allow for renegotiations on debt packages to take place. It is not difficult to see why the credit rating agencies are being vilified for their actions. However, it is important that we see all sides to the picture. What position are the credit rating agencies in?

Let us for a moment leave aside the question of moral duty and look closer at whether the system in place now would even allow for more intervention from the agencies. Yuefen Li, in her UN report, concludes with this suggestion:

> Suspend the issuance of ratings during a crisis when there are international efforts to introduce mechanisms to deal with the crisis. In times of crisis, rating agencies should defer publishing their rating reviews, as markets have their way of discounting risk when fundamentals are conspicuously changing. In addition, rating announcements could hamper the implementation of special crisis containment and resolution measures introduced by the international community. Not suspending credit ratings during this kind of situation would compromise international efforts.[70]

Technically, this is not possible for a number of reasons. First, according to the legal frameworks that govern the rating agencies, primarily in the US and the EU, a credit rating agency cannot simply stop issuing credit ratings. Furthermore, after the EU sovereign debt crisis in the aftermath of the Financial Crisis, the EU made it abundantly clear in its regulations that essentially, a credit rating agency must say what it does and do what it says. Any deviation from stated methodologies and approaches would open the agencies up to liability, and the credit rating agencies are adept at avoiding liability. Second, requesting that credit rating agencies suspend their ratings ignores the reality of the relationship between the credit rating agencies and private investors. The most resourced and influential investors are institutional investors (some are even considered to be 'universal owners', meaning their reach spans entire economies), and they have a particular constitution; they are investing other people's and institutions' money. With that being the case, credit ratings play a key role in regulating the actions of those investors (both internally and externally), and removing the ratings from the process would hinder that structure irrevocably. Furthermore, entering into an investment on the basis of a credit rating and then that rating being forcibly removed affects the investment environment beyond compare. Lastly, it would be without precedent, and the uncertainty would result in a lack of progressive action from the private investors; the likelihood would be that they would request to have their debt agreements settled immediately to protect themselves from the new and uncertain environment.

The legal element is the key, and we will come to this in the penultimate chapter. However, it is worth putting forward a simple explainer of the underlying dynamics affecting the credit rating industry and everything it is associated with. That can be done by describing a theory that I have applied to the credit rating dynamic on several occasions: signalling theory.

Signalling theory is a widely applied theory that rests upon a simple construct: 'signalling theory is concerned with how and why organisms exchange otherwise hidden information about each other or the world around them'.[71] It is clear to see why it has been widely applied. Usually, the proposed process of signalling involves a signaller, who has the information they need to share or convince others of, sending a signal to the receiver. The receiver then interprets the signal and by engaging (or not) with that signaller provides feedback to the signaller. This is the usual process, but it does not fit the credit rating situation because this would mean the issuer merely tells the investor that they are creditworthy, and the investor chooses whether to invest. We know that this is not how investments work; thus, in a recent work, I amended the process to fit the credit rating situation:

- Signaller (a person, product, or firm that has an underlying quality and needs to convince others of it)
- The information on the underlying quality is sent to a third party
- The third party assesses the quality of the signal and sends its own signal to the receiver
- The receiver observes and interprets the third party's signal and chooses to absorb the signal
- Feedback is sent to the signaller via investment (in whatever form)[72]

To provide more context, Wolf explains the underlying sentiment of the theory:

> In its essence, signalling theory is about information asymmetry, defined as one side knowing more than the other side . . . this information asymmetry causes uncertainty on the receiver side regarding quality, service, characteristics, qualifications, etc. and uncertainty is related to higher information costs and higher perceptions of risk. Signalling theory highlights two types of information, information about quality and information about intent. In the first case, one side has no complete information on the characteristics of the other side. In the second case, one side is not fully aware of the behaviour or the intentions of another party.[73]

Theoretically, for the credit rating signalling to work, one key ingredient must be present: trust. The investor needs to trust that the rating agency is adequately independent of the issuer, and the investor needs to trust in the capability of the rating agency to accurately represent the riskiness of the information provided to it by the issuer in a standardised form, that is, the investor needs to trust that AAA-rated security is exactly that. This is the theory. However, the facts that credit rating agencies derive their income – in the art of ratings, at least – from the issuer and that the credit rating agencies were found to have knowingly conspired *against* the investors in the Financial Crisis has had no material effect on their usage nor success; in fact, the rating agencies have grown considerably larger and wealthier since the Financial Crisis. Therefore, something must be amiss about the theoretical importance of the rating agencies.

The answer to the usefulness of the rating agencies can be found in the concept of signalling but in a different manner to the theoretical construct of signalling theory; it is the utility of signalling that is important. For example, the majority of impactful investment in the modern age is done by institutional or 'sophisticated' investors, with the art of 'retail' or 'unsophisticated' investing now becoming a dying artform. Most retail investors now invest in indices or in larger investors. This changes the dynamic of investing and moves it towards a relationship where multi-directional signalling is required. I, say, as a small-time investor or pension-holder may want to signal to the management of my investor that they can only invest in certain categories of investment aligned to accepted risk frameworks. The easiest method of risk assessment to understand is the credit rating, with its simple and (theoretically) widely understood alphanumeric system – C-rated securities are riskier than AA-rated securities, to provide a crude example. It could also be the case that an institutional investor declares to new investors that they would only invest in securities rated B and above to entice investors with particular risk appetites, for example. It is also widely understood that regulators will determine which investment categories particular industries can invest in, in relation to their interrelationship with society; for example, pension funds are usually prohibited from being involved in anything lower than A-rated securities because of the nature of the money they are investing, whereas hedge funds may operate within the lower ends of the rating scale because they are not widely regulated and the people and organisations' resources they are investing have a much higher appetite for risk. In the sovereign space, sovereigns align to this often too, with press announcements about the strength of one's credit rating being developed to signal strength to its own voting public and its competitors. The beauty of credit rating is its apparent simplicity and the widely recognisable nature of its rating symbols.

You can see from the above discussion why simply stopping or suspending ratings is not possible. The breakdown in underlying communication between a host of different parties would cause the investing machine to grind to a halt and make things immeasurably worse. One aspect that this book does want to promote is the concept of finding a progressive solution for the countries, not just an immediate one. Whilst an immediate resolution is absolutely necessary, it is the same approach that was taken by the debt treatment initiatives over the past 50 or so years. The chances are considerably high that a short-term resolution such as suspending credit ratings or pushing the idea that sovereign states should simply default and come back to the capital markets when they are ready may work in the very short-term but may cause the continuation or even the worsening of problems long into the future. That is why the solution put forward in the next chapter seeks to utilise this understanding of the underlying dynamics of the credit rating impasse to develop a proposal that can have long-lasting effects. However, before that, let us finish our linear analysis of the debt treatment initiatives being developed by looking at the new *Common Framework* that the G20 has tried to implement.

3.5 The Common Framework on Debt Treatment Beyond the DSSI

The 'Common Framework', as it is known, was developed by the G20 to act as a follow-on debt treatment initiative after the DSSI was brought to a conclusion. The DSSI came to an end at the very end of 2021, after a short extension. Now, countries seeking debt relief (either via reductions in cases or through postponements of debt payments and/or servicing payment deferrals) must do so via the Common Framework. The Common Framework is similar to the DSSI that came before it, except for two key differences.

First, the Common Framework has the backing of more of the G20, not just the Paris Club. This time, China, Turkey, India, and Saudi Arabia are part of the plan. This broadens the scope of the potential relief that can be made from working on official debt. However, in an expected but telling twist, the G20 is *insisting* that debtor countries seek *comparable debt treatment* from their private creditors if they are to participate in the Common Framework. This is the G20's attempt to address the glaring issue affecting the DSSI. The only question needed now then is whether they have been successful.

It should come as no surprise, especially based on the analysis we have undertaken in this book so far and especially in this chapter, that the answer is an unequivocal 'no'. This is because rather than try and alter some of the underlying dynamics that prevented private creditor participation in the DSSI, the G20 has instead 'doubled down'. It is questionable what the aim was with this decision because the only effect has been to force the underlying dynamic into the light, and it is proving costly. It is leading to numerous criticisms, even from those closely connected to the scheme. The First Deputy Managing Director of the IMF, Gita Gopinath, said in early January 2022 that 'a lot more is needed to actually get it to deliver on its promise',[74] with World Bank Chief David Malpass noting just a week earlier that 'debt relief is much needed for the poorer countries. If we wait too long, it will be too late'.[75] Malpass called for the inclusion of aggregative CACs to be included in all sovereign bond sales, but this is not particularly helpful as there is no legal framework to accommodate this and they could not be retroactive. Continuing, Rebeca Grynspan, Secretary-General of the UN Conference on Trade and Development said recently regarding the Common Framework and the insistence on comparable treatment, 'you know what it means for a country to say publicly it has problems paying its debts . . . the private sector will punish them. If a country has any choice, it won't do it'.[76]

On this point, the credit rating agencies have been emphatically clear. Ethiopia is one of only three countries that approached the scheme for inclusion, and it was immediately downgraded as a result. Fitch Ratings, in announcing the downgrade, said that 'Fitch Ratings believes that a decision to seek debt restructuring under the Common Framework for Debt Treatments announced last November by the G20 and the Paris Club is unlikely to be compatible with a rating higher than "CCC". This has been reflected in our decision to downgrade Ethiopia's rating to 'CCC' from 'B/Negative'.[77] As if there was any doubt, the rating agencies were true to their word because as we saw in the last section, they have to be in this instance. Fitch continues that although there are scenarios whereby the Common Framework would not automatically lead to default ratings for subscribing sovereigns – an exemption being made for private sector involvement, for example – this would be very unlikely indeed, mostly because it would make the Common Framework simply an extension of the DSSI, which is not the Common Framework's aim. Therefore, the agency clarifies that:

> Further evidence that a sovereign will be accessing CF treatment associated with private-sector restructuring could lead to a downgrade to 'CC', meaning a default is 'probable'. The publication of a consent solicitation for bondholders could lead to a downgrade to 'C', and its acceptance a further move to Restricted Default, 'RD'. The rating would be upgraded to a level reflecting its post-restructuring fundamentals shortly thereafter.[78]

Some have downplayed the significance of what appears to be an automatic downgrading to default if a sovereign applies and successfully gets to the trigger point in the Common Framework. We know already that some have called for countries to default if necessary, and this is supported by others such as the Executive Secretary of the UN Economic Commission for Africa, Vera Songwe, who said that 'you can't have your cake and eat it at the same time', continuing that 'those that need a debt restructuring have to call it that and say so because there is too much stigma around the issue'.[79] This may indeed be the case, and it presents a stark choice for sovereigns because the rating agencies are clear that 'any material change of terms for private creditors, including the lowering of coupons or the extension of maturities, would be consistent with the definition of default'.[80]

Regrettably, there is not much more to say on the Common Framework. It is the most recent debt treatment initiative and, unfortunately, not much has happened since it was launched. The countries that have attempted to join (Chad, Ethiopia, and Zambia) are stuck in no man's land, awaiting rescue from the multilateral institutions, and it is questionable whether that is even forthcoming. At the time of writing, the IMF suggested that they will be aiming to arrange a memorandum of understanding with all of Chad's creditors by late March 2022,[81] which would be nearly 12 months since Chad applied to join.[82] The Jubilee Debt Campaign suggested that this case is a litmus test for the G20's credibility on debt treatment for vulnerable countries, but one wonders whether we are seeing the results of that test before our eyes.

The Common Framework is a lazy attempt at debt treatment. The world saw the lack of effect on the private creditor space from the DSSI, and for some reason, the G20 decided to try it again with no work being put in to understand and change the underlying dynamic. They will pay the same price, but more importantly, it is the vulnerable sovereigns and their citizens who will pay the biggest price of all. Work must be done to alter that underlying dynamic in a progressive manner if any good is to come from this awful mess. We will now work through the book's proposed plan, which is different from any of the short-term 'fixes' that have been suggested.

3.6 Conclusion

The DSSI, as representing the best efforts of the international elite to alleviate the pressure being faced by the world's most vulnerable countries, missed the mark. Earlier in the book, we saw how the MDRI attempted to build on the HIPC initiative and essentially wipe the slate clean of official debt whilst also incorporating key performance indicators that would lead to much stronger economies. That approach was welcome and, more importantly, was working well. Vulnerable countries were steadily growing stronger. Yet, it was too late in the day because what awaited those vulnerable countries was a once-in-a-generation global pandemic that would shine a light on all of the structural inefficiencies that were woven into the relatively modern sovereign states.

The lack of a solid structure, based on sovereign states that were left hamstrung when the colonialists decided to move to a more economic model of control, is clear for all to see. The states only had 10, 15, or 20 years before they were forced into crises by market conditions, which is not long enough to establish solid economic fundamentals. Since then, the states have been fighting economic fires, and misdirected debt treatment initiatives fanned the flames. The success of the HIPC and MDRI initiatives should have stood as models for future debt treatment and moved the leading developed nations away from us-first models of debt treatment to you-first. That is what was required for the countries as they faced the global pandemic. Instead, increasing global protectionism and nationalism came to the fore, and the vulnerable were left without adequate protection from the health and financial aspects of the pandemic.

In this chapter, we saw how there are underlying dynamics within the debt arena that cannot be ignored. The growing influence of the private sector brings with it particular dynamics that must be factored into any debt treatment initiative; we now know that with the DSSI and the Common Framework, this was not the case. Understanding the intricacies of the power dynamics that bind private investors, as just one example, would surely tell even the most uninitiated person that demanding comparable debt treatment between the official and private creditors would not work, and yet the G20 has persisted. The actions of the IIF are perhaps unpalatable but perfectly reasonable. In a purely analytical sense, the position of their members is getting riskier with the official announcement, and they would not be a trade body if they did not represent the interests of their members. The same argument goes for the credit rating agencies who, having been labelled morally obtuse by some, are simply doing their job. Not only is it their job to reflect the risks faced by private investors in their ratings, but they are also *legally bound* to do so. The opening of the legal floodgates in terms of liability could be catastrophic for the agencies if they were to change their stated models and methodologies and then private creditors incurred serious losses. What we are faced with is a systemic issue.

However, calling for systemic change is useful, but not particularly helpful in this instance. Now is arguably not the time to be embarking on significant structural change. Some have called for a public credit rating agency to be set up, but this is difficult because of liability issues and moral hazards. In reality, all that is needed is gentle and progressive structural amendments. There need to be slight nudges to ease the credit rating impasse, and this is what this book will now call for. There exists an opportunity to move the credit rating agencies from a prohibitive position to a facilitative one. However, to do that, certain 'pillars' of the financial system will need to make small moves to make it happen.

Notes

1 Brahima Sangafowa Coulibaly, Dhruv Gandhi, and Lemma W. Senbet, 'Debt Sustainability and Financing for Development: A Key Post-Covid Challenge' (2021) *Brookings Institute* (Feb 9) www.brookings.edu/blog/africa-in-focus/2021/02/09/debt-sustainability-and-financing-for-development-a-key-post-covid-challenge/.
2 World Bank, *International Debt Statistics 2021* (2021) https://openknowledge.worldbank.org/bitstream/handle/10986/34588/9781464816109.pdf?sequence=4&isAllowed=y 15.
3 Ibid.
4 Ibid 17.
5 Saad Hasan, 'Will Zambia be Able to Stand Up to Private Creditors?' (2020) *TRTWorld* (Oct 2) www.trtworld.com/magazine/will-zambia-be-able-to-stand-up-to-private-creditors-40200.
6 Eurodad, *The G20 Debt Service Suspension Initiative: Draining out the Titanic with a Bucket?* (2020) https://d3n8a8pro7vhmx.cloudfront.net/eurodad/pages/768/attachments/original/1610121986/DSSI-briefing-final.pdf?1610121986 2.
7 Ibid.
8 Ibid 2.2.
9 Ibid.
10 S&P, 'G20 Sovereign Debt Suspension: To Apply, or Not to Apply' (2020) (Dec 1) www.spglobal.com/ratings/en/research/articles/201201-g20-sovereign-debt-suspension-to-apply-or-not-to-apply-11750938.
11 Ibid.
12 Ibid.
13 Ben Parker, 'The Debt Crisis Looming for Poor Countries' (2020) *The New Humanitarian* (Oct 8) www.thenewhumanitarian.org/analysis/2020/10/08/pandemic-debt-crisis-looms.
14 Ibid.
15 Charles Panati, *Panati's Extraordinary Origins of Everyday Things* (Book Sales 2016) 187.
16 Miryam Vander Stichele, *The IIF & Debt Relief* (SOMO 2021) 24.
17 Patrick Bolton, Lee Buchelt, Pierre-Olivier Gourinchas, Mitu Gulati, Chang-Tai Hsieh, Ugo Panizza, and Beatrice Weder di Mauro, 'Sovereign Debt Standstills: An Update' (2020) *VoxEU* (May 28) https://voxeu.org/article/sovereign-debt-standstills-update.
18 Stichele (n 16).
19 Ibid.
20 Ibid 26.
21 Ibid.

22 IIF, 'Terms of Reference for Voluntary Private Sector Participation in the G20/ Paris Club DSSI' (2020) *IIF* (May 28) www.iif.com/Publications/ID/3920/Terms-of-Reference-for-Voluntary-Private-Sector-Participation-in-the-G20Paris-Club-DSSI.
23 Stichele (n 16) 27.
24 Bolton et al. (n 17).
25 Kraemer, the former head of S&P's sovereign ratings division, is a strong supporter of the argument that market access would not be as harmed as the narrative suggests, were a country to default. See Moritz Kraemer, 'Bondholders Need to Forgive Some African Sovereign Debt' (2020) *Financial Times* (Aug 27) www.ft.com/content/7d93235c-ffea-44bc-a0f0-fa1de09012b3.
26 Cameroon serves as an interesting case study in this regard. See Jurgen Kaiser and Elise Kopper, 'Debt Relief? Thanks, but No Thanks!' (2020) *IPS* (Sep 28) www.ips-journal.eu/topics/foreign-and-security-policy/debt-relief-thanks-but-no-thanks-4671/.
27 Bolton et al. (n 17).
28 Marc Jones, 'Poorest Countries Face Tough Choice over G20 Debt Relief Plan' (2020) *Reuters* (Sep 30) www.reuters.com/article/health-coronavirus-g20debtrelief-analysi-idUSKBN26L2N3.
29 Parker (n 13).
30 Stichele (n 16) 37.
31 Bolton et al. (n 17).
32 World Bank (2) 12.
33 Parker (n 13).
34 Ibid.
35 Bruno Macaes, *Belt and Road: A Chinese World Order* (OUP 2021); Jeremy Garlick, *The Impact of China's Belt and Road Initiative: From Asia to Europe* (Routledge 2019).
36 World Bank (n 2) 7.
37 Dipanjan Chaudhury, 'Africa's Rising Debt: Chinese Loans to Continent Exceeds $140 Billion' (2021) *Economic Times* (Sept 23) https://economictimes.indiatimes.com/news/international/world-news/africas-rising-debt-chinese-loans-to-continent-exceeds-140-billion/articleshow/86444602.cms?from=mdr.
38 Jonathan Wheatley, 'Borrow to Fight Economic Impact of Pandemic, Says World Bank's Chief Economist' (2020) *Financial Times* (Oct 8) www.ft.com/content/0582e495-765a-46a1-98f9-ac48e80a139c.
39 David Rogovic, Matt Robinson, Marie Diron, and Alastair Wilson, 'More Dispersed Creditor Base Across SSA Countries Complicates Potential Debt Restructuring Negotiations' in Moody's, *Sovereign Monitor: Impact of Coronavirus on Sub-Saharan Africa, November 2020* (2020) www.moodys.com/researchdocumentcontentpage.aspx?docid=PBC_1246395 4.
40 Ibid.
41 TRT World, 'China Denies Claims of Trapping Africa Countries in Debt' (2022) *TRT World* (Jan 7) www.trtworld.com/africa/china-denies-claims-of-trapping-africa-countries-in-debt-53393.
42 Daniel Large, *China and Africa: The New Era* (John Wiley & Sons 2021) 1.
43 Moody's, *Emerging Markets Insight* (2020) (Dec) www.moodys.com/researchdocumentcontentpage.aspx?docid=PBC_1252416.
44 S&P, 'G20 Sovereign Debt Suspension: To Apply, or Not to Apply' (2020) (Dec 1) www.spglobal.com/ratings/en/research/articles/201201-g20-sovereign-debt-suspension-to-apply-or-not-to-apply-11750938.
45 Development Reimagined, *Options for Reimagining Africa's Debt System* (2021) https://heyzine.com/flip-book/981ad6e913.html#page/1 17.
46 Coulibaly et al. (n 1) 12.
47 Alex Vines, 'China's Southern Africa Debt Deals Reveal a Wider Plan' (2020) *Chatham House* (Dec 10) www.chathamhouse.org/2020/12/chinas-southern-africa-debt-deals-reveal-wider-plan.

48 Ibid.
49 World Bank, *Global Development Finance: Striving for Stability in Development Finance* (World Bank 2003) 63.
50 Antonio Sainz de Vicuna y Barraso, 'Identical Collective Action Clauses for Different Legal Systems: A European Model' in Patrick S. Kenadijan, Klaus-Albert Bauer, and Andreas Cahn, *Collective Action Clauses and the Restructuring of Sovereign Debt* (Walter de Gruyter 2013) 19.
51 Christian Kopf, 'Sovereign Debt Restructuring: Lessons from History' in Patrick S. Kenadijan, Klaus-Albert Bauer, and Andreas Cahn, *Collective Action Clauses and the Restructuring of Sovereign Debt* (Walter de Gruyter 2013) 158.
52 Barraso (n 49) 16.
53 A 'spread' simply refers to the price paid by the investor in comparison to a particular benchmark.
54 Barraso (n 49).
55 World Bank (n 48).
56 Ibid.
57 Kopf (n 50) 161.
58 Anna Gelpern, 'The Importance of Being Standard' (2017) *Georgetown University Law Center*. https://scholarship.law.georgetown.edu/cgi/viewcontent.cgi?article=2989&context=facpub 23.
59 Kopf (n 50) 161.
60 Ibid 165.
61 Steven L. Schwarz, 'Sovereign Debt Restructuring and English Governing Law' (2017) 12 *Brooklyn Journal of Corporate, Financial and Commercial Law* 73–103, 74.
62 Ibid 76.
63 Nicole Kearse, 'The DSSI, Defaults and Credit Ratings: A Primer' (2020) *ALSF* (June 26) https://alsf.academy/blog/dssi-defaults-and-credit-ratings-primer.
64 Ibid.
65 Ibid.
66 Camilla Hodgson, 'Moody's Clashes with UN Over G20 Debt-Relief Efforts' (2020) *Financial Times* (July 21) www.ft.com/content/7d51d373-c12e-4440-a408-e61a939e3a3c.
67 Jayati Ghosh, 'Credit-Rating Agencies Could Derail Economic Recovery' (2021) *The Jordan Times* (Apr 7) www.jordantimes.com/opinion/jayati-ghosh/credit-rating-agencies-could-derail-economic-recovery.
68 UN, *Debt Relief, Debt Crisis Prevention and Human Rights: The Role of Credit Rating Agencies* (2021) https://undocs.org/A/HRC/46/29.
69 Bolton et al. (n 17) emphasis added.
70 UN (n 67) 18.
71 Douglas W. Bird and Rebecca Bliege Bird, 'Signalling Theory and Durable Symbolic Expression' in Bruno David and Ian J. McNiven, *The Oxford Handbook of the Archaeology and Anthropology of Rock Art* (OUP 2019) 347.
72 Daniel Cash, *Sustainability Rating Agencies vs Credit Rating Agencies: The Battle for the Mainstream Investor* (Palgrave Macmillan 2021) 99.
73 Sandra Wolf, *Signaling Family Firm Identity: Family Firm Identification and its Effects on Job Seekers' Perceptions about a Potential Employer* (Springer 2017) 32.
74 Andrea Shalal and David Lawder, 'IMF's Gopinath Says "A Lot More Work" Needed to Help Countries Cut Debt Risks' (2022) *Reuters* (Jan 25) www.reuters.com/markets/rates-bonds/imfs-gopinath-says-a-lot-more-work-needed-help-countries-cut-debt-risks-2022-01-25/.
75 Karin Strohecker and Andrea Shalal, 'World Bank Demands Faster G20 Debt Relief as Poor Nations Squeezed' (2022) *Reuters* (Jan 11) www.reuters.com/markets/europe/world-bank-demands-faster-g20-debt-relief-poor-nations-squeezed-2022-01-11/.
76 Jonathan Wheatley, 'Poorest Countries Face $11bn Surge in Debt Repayments' (2022) *Financial Times* (Jan 17) www.ft.com/content/4b5f4b54-2f80-4bda-9df7-9e74a3c8a66a.

77 Fitch Ratings, 'Common Framework Access Could Lead to Sovereign Debt Default' (2021) *Fitch Ratings* (Feb 16) www.fitchratings.com/research/sovereigns/common-framework-access-could-lead-to-sovereign-debt-default-16-02-2021.
78 Ibid.
79 Macau Business, 'Angola: Only Country to Restructure Private Debt without Rating Downgrade – UN' (2021) *Macau Business* (Mar 22) www.macaubusiness.com/angola-only-country-to-restructure-private-debt-without-rating-downgrade-un/.
80 Fitch, 'Fitch Downgrades Ethiopia to "CCC"' (2021) *Fitch* (Feb 9) www.fitchratings.com/research/sovereigns/fitch-downgrades-ethiopia-to-ccc-09-02-2021.
81 Andrea Shalal and Karin Strohecker, 'IMF to Meet with Chad's Creditors by End of January, Spokesperson Says' (2022) *Reuters* (Jan 24) www.reuters.com/world/africa/imf-meet-with-all-chads-creditors-by-end-january-spokesperson-2022-01-24/.
82 Jubilee Debt campaign, 'Decision Time for Chad's Private Creditors and the Common Framework' (2021) *Jubilee Debt Campaign* (July 1) https://jubileedebt.org.uk/blog/decision-time-for-chads-private-creditors-and-the-common-framework.

4 Resolving the Credit Rating Impasse

Part One

4.1 Introduction

In 2021, myself and several colleagues from across the world developed the first stage of a two-stage solution to resolving the credit rating impasse. In this chapter, I will detail the first stage of the project's proposals.[1] The second stage follows in the next chapter with a legal analysis that, as proposed, can tie everything together and provide for a framework where the adjustment to breach the credit rating impasse can be realised. However, before that, there is a three-pronged approach that puts in place a foundation for a progressive solution to the standstill that is currently affecting the world's most vulnerable countries.

In proposing such solutions, there is a need to tackle the problem in a variety of ways. If the proposal's aim is to generate a longer-term and more progressive solution, then there are multiple points that need to be addressed. As we saw in previous chapters, the recent initiatives aim to keep things the same as much as possible and provide a short and sharp solution. What is presented here is very different and will need political and general will to push for substantive changes for the better. This can be considered a 'structural adjustment' for the modern debt system. Essentially, the aim is to acknowledge and accept the sticking points in the credit rating dynamic and then evolve those sticking points so that the system can become more facilitative.

However, it is not a complete story; it cannot be. The proposal develops elements that only the particular 'pillars' can address. For example, the proposal develops a space for the credit rating agencies to change their rating approaches and methodologies where sovereigns are concerned. However, it does not dictate precisely what those should look like. That can only be done in *collaboration* with other stakeholders, including the sovereigns and private creditors (and their representative bodies, such as the IIF). Furthermore, it does begin a process which is analogous to the concept of structural adjustment. It does this because the newly proposed credit rating system would *actively reward* countries for developing particular indicators, thus developing those crucial sectors of the countries' economies and transforming the nature of the credit rating agency in the sovereign space. So, there are a lot of moving parts.

DOI: 10.4324/9781003261223-5

It is necessary to present such ideas as this because there is a distinct lack of long-term thinking being displayed on the global scene. I say this with two caveats attached; one being that I am not suggesting that this proposal here is the only one worth considering, and the other being that the other proposals and ideas that have been put forward – whether shorter- or longer-term – are certainly worth considering. There are certainly merits in each idea put forward by very intelligent and committed people. The question we asked ourselves as a group, however, is what is the goal? The setting of a goal in this field can absolutely dictate the scope of success. Our aim was very long-term indeed. Whilst this proposal can, if implemented, positively affect the credit rating impasse, it is also designed for future instances. Its aim, essentially, was to resolve the debt treatment issue concerning private creditors, which will undoubtedly affect vulnerable countries well beyond the COVID-19 pandemic.

Whilst the proposal does not directly resolve the issue regarding the lack of a bankruptcy procedure on the sovereign scene, in a way it could. The presence of the multilateral institutions (usually prompted by the group of leading countries) with regards to debt treatment means there is potential to rely on them being a party in any given scalable debt treatment initiative. With their lead, as imagined by this proposal, they could set the parameters for the credit rating agencies to apply the temporary models we envisage whenever there is a global need; this, essentially, resolves the need for a bankruptcy mechanism whenever there is a systemic risk, rather than on a country-by-country singular basis. However, there are limitations. This proposal provides for more flexibility for credit rating agencies, which is contentious. I do not advocate for the deregulation of credit rating agencies – far from it – but for the re-regulation of credit rating agencies, which in itself is a sensitive issue at a time when regulators and legislators are keen to establish as much control as possible over this historically unregulated sector. It also calls for private initiatives to be developed to support countries in their financial matters, which would not be without its challenges; countries may not want to pay for such services or may need convincing of their worth, and numerous associated legal issues would be encountered in providing the right and protective environment that would be needed. At this stage, however, the idea is in place.

4.2 Private Creditor Support

Private creditor support for this idea is crucial. The original idea was to have a 'waiver' of sorts, such as that developed by the IIF for the DSSI, but this is not an absolute necessity. A waiver is not necessary because there is no bond between the private creditors and the credit rating agencies like there is between the private creditors and the sovereign debtors, who would require such waivers if they were to restructure their debt agreements. Between the credit rating agencies and private creditors, there simply exists the potential for litigation for the recovery of losses, like that witnessed in the aftermath of the Financial Crisis. In this sovereign sector, the credit rating agencies could only alter their methodologies and approach with legislative/regulatory support, meaning there would be no avenue for litigation unless the credit rating agencies stepped outside of what was agreed in the amendments; the rating agencies would not have any financial incentive to do this, like they did have in the structured finance market that was at the centre of the Financial Crisis.

Therefore, that support could come in the form of a letter of support from trade bodies and individual investors in the sovereign space. To achieve this, the development of the larger plan would need to incorporate the views of the private creditor space. It would need to do this so that the proposed rating model, and what it aimed to promote, were part of a much larger 'push' to develop better quality debtors. As we shall see in the next section, there is now a need to push for better incorporation of ESG-based ideals and, particularly, climate-related ideals within the development of the developing world. Many have and are calling for the developing world to be aided in combatting climate change because they do not have the resources to be expected to fight with and because it is predominantly the developing world that is most affected by climate-related issues.[2] This proposal can directly help with that problem. It also has the capacity, by injecting ESG and climate change directly into the aims of the project, to bring in a new wave of sustainable-based investment that can have a transformative effect on the developing world.

There are elements to the original IIF waiver which would be translated into the newly imagined rating process. For example, the IIF discuss, in relation to their waiver, that 'countries that have employed the combination of good policies, good communication, and disclosure practices . . . have been able to maintain investor confidence and have performed better relative to others'.[3] As we shall see, good communication with one's creditors and better disclosure practices, as determined through transparency elements within the multilateral initiative framework, are factored into the new and temporary rating methodology to encourage better practices.

Ultimately, the private creditor space would have a lot of incentive to support this broad idea. The proposal does not dictate how the private creditors would renegotiate their debt deals with the sovereigns, and nor would it mandate that restructuring must take place; in the end, it may not be in the best interests of the creditors to renegotiate. However, we must take the private creditors at their word and the IIF, as their seemingly representative body, has confirmed that private creditors *do* want to get involved with alleviating debt pressures; it is just that the countries are not coming forward (because of the credit rating impasse). If this is removed, then making the path to renegotiation as simple as possible should encourage private creditors to get involved.

4.3 A New Way to (Temporarily) Rate Sovereign Debt

The previous section was short because not much is needed technically from the private creditors. The support of their sector for this proposed plan would be influential and provide for more opportunities to feed their views into the plan, but that is it. However, the idea of changing the manner in which credit rating agencies rate sovereign states is no small feat. Interestingly, there is an internal precedent for applying an 'overlay' on top of normal rating procedures. In this section, we shall review one of those instances where an 'overlay' is applied, and spell out the proposed 'overlay'.

However, before we do that, there is a shortcut that could be applied. The purpose of proposing the overlay which will follow shortly is to inject a sense of progressiveness into the rating process, whereby it no longer exists as an opinion on creditworthiness but as a vehicle for change within the targeted sector (vulnerable nations) without changing or diluting (or increasing, perhaps) the role of the credit rating agencies, which would not be palatable for the credit rating agencies. That shortcut has its origins in the aftermath of the Financial Crisis and could be easily applied as long as it had legislative/regulatory backing like the post-Financial Crisis amendment in the rating scale approaches did.

In 2008, as the scale of the Financial Crisis was slowly revealing itself, the International Organisation of Securities Commissions produced a consultation report entitled 'The Role of Credit Rating Agencies in Structured Finance Markets'.[4] The report mentioned:

> In this connection, a large number of the Technical Committee members are minded to call for CRAs to differentiate the ratings of structured finance products from corporate debt ratings in order to provide investors with an additional signal about possible differences in how those different types of securities may perform under different stress scenarios. Consequently, as part of the consultation process, the Technical Committee seeks public comment on the desirability of using a different set of rating symbols to differentiate structured finance ratings from ratings of corporate debt securities.[5]

In response, major financial bodies responded that it was generally a good idea to have differentiating symbols within the rating scales so that investors knew immediately that the traditional rating procedures that one could *legally* expect to be followed in the corporate rating sector, for example, may be different in the field of structured finance ratings. There was precedent for this to be done, as the Association of Corporate Treasurers, in their public response to the consultation, explained:

> CRAs necessarily use different methodologies in rating different types of instruments/issuers and in subsequent monitoring. Here, this may mean that that a rating of a structured product can be qualitatively different from that of a corporate or sovereign security. If it is not obvious, this may be deduced, from CRAs' methodology descriptions. Certain CRAs in rating money market funds draw attention to the different methodology in rating and frequency and mode of monitoring by using a suffix letter – as AAAm, etc. – and this is very effective. We think that this provides a good model

> for structured credits. So, the CRAs should consider appending a simple suffix for structured finance ratings, e.g. AAAsf, to guide investors and other market participants towards referring to the specific approach taken in evaluating the particular type of structured finance.[6]

In the US, it was being debated whether credit rating agency rating scales and symbols should be standardised to make the process of understanding the ratings simpler. Not surprisingly, but quite correctly, both the market and the credit rating agencies were against this idea. The main reasons for being against the idea were that each rating agency rates differently; thus, comparing across the scales is not helpful at best and wrong at worst. Similarly, as Moody's made clear, any rules requiring standardisation 'likely would interfere with the independence of the rating process by regulating the substance of rating opinions and methodologies', which the SEC is simply not allowed to do as the Mortgage Bankers Association questioned when they stated that 'the introduction of standardised terminology would go beyond the statutory authority of the Dodd–Frank Act by prescribing elements of the rating methodology'. Furthermore, S&P responded that 'regulatory mandates concerning what ratings must mean and how credit rating agencies go about their work also raise serious First Amendment concerns'.[7]

However, market participants were keen on the idea of attaching a differentiating symbol to ratings for structured finance; the Mortgage Insurance Companies of America said that there should be separate symbols for structured finance ratings as 'failure to differentiate ratings for structured finance would repeat history, in which certain structured instruments were represented as largely consisting of a single asset class or risk bucket, but in fact resulted in very different risk'.[8] Nevertheless, the US was way behind the curve with regards to this matter.

In the EU, in their first-of-three pieces of major legislation on the rating agencies, Article 10.3 declared:

> When a credit rating agency issues credit ratings for structured finance instruments, it shall ensure that rating categories that are attributed to structured finance instruments are clearly differentiated using an additional symbol which distinguishes them from rating categories used for any other entities, financial instruments or financial obligations.[9]

The EU responded to the suggestions from the umbrella IOSCO on this matter. Instantly, the force of the legislation was recognised, and all three major credit rating agencies adopted the 'sf' additional suffix for their structured finance ratings.[10] S&P led the way, declaring that its adoption of 'sf' would be global as it would be the most practical approach.[11] Eventually, other credit rating agencies, though not all, adopted similar measures.[12]

This is now common practice in the rating industry as it was pushed through via legislation. Even if the US has not legislated in the same direction, it is deemed good practice and, as S&P noted, it makes sense to roll it out globally so as not to cause unnecessary confusion, which they have done. Therefore, the same could be applied here. Applying a rating signifier is not tampering with the independence or the methodologies of the rating agencies. However, if it were applied in the sovereign space to allow for sovereigns to renegotiate with their private creditors, it may not be as simple as the 'sf' signifier and would, therefore, need legislative backing (which will be proposed in the next chapter). This is because whilst, say, a simple 'CF' signifier for any sovereign that is engaging in the Common Framework would serve the purpose of indicating to investors that the credit rating agencies are aware that the sovereign is seeking to renegotiate its debts with private creditors and that the subscription to the Common Framework means that it is agreed it has credit-positive potential and it has agreed that entry into the Common Framework would not mean an automatic default rating (as long as the country in question did not deserve a default rating, which may not always be the case). This is why the stated support of the private creditors, which would then be backed up by legislation to protect the credit rating agencies from liability, would be necessary. Importantly, the credit rating agencies would only be protected from not issuing default ratings automatically; any malfeasance on their behalf would still be open to liability.

As you can see, it is possible but complicated. It takes the will of several moving parts. The most important is the legislative background because, as we saw in relation to the EU legislation, it is what is needed to move the dial forward in any given direction. Quite rightly, but also because of their unique history, the credit rating agencies are particularly aware of their exposure to liability and fight tooth and nail to shield themselves. Therefore, the legal protection for them, in relation to this *temporary* plan, would need to be crystal clear. This shortcut could break the impasse. However, we also designed an 'overlay' that could boost the Common Framework's impact over and above providing for fiscal assistance.

To reiterate, the solution being put forward here has three components. The first is to have private creditors support the idea of a temporary rating mechanism attached to the Common Framework (or another multilateral initiative) which still contains the potential for a country to be downgraded to default status. The second stage (minus the potential shortcut detailed above) is to have the credit rating agencies decide on a framework that could be applied to countries attached to the multilateral initiative. Whilst a blanket methodology would be beneficial, there is a constant claim from credit rating agencies that their independence must be protected so that they could achieve the objectives of the solution and create their own versions of the 'overlay', but everything would need to be transparent; this should not be an issue because transparency of methodological development is mandated by statute. Details of the types of elements that should be considered in an 'overlay' are presented in the subsequent text. That leaves the final stage, which would be for advisory services to be established in the private sector to aid sovereigns in building up their fundamentals and repairing relationships with credit rating agencies and creditors.

Before we look at the overlay, it is worth illustrating (Figures 4.1 and 4.2)[13] how the process could work and why it would be beneficial.

There is precedent for the application of a 'rating overlay', albeit in a different context. For example, whilst an array of financial institutions (FIs) have been deploying 'qualitative overlays' to supplement core quantitative models for years,[14] Fitch Ratings recently spelt out how they have developed and applied a qualitative overlay (QO) to the sovereign rating space. Fitch's QO is designed to reflect the subjectivity of the many different elements that may impact a

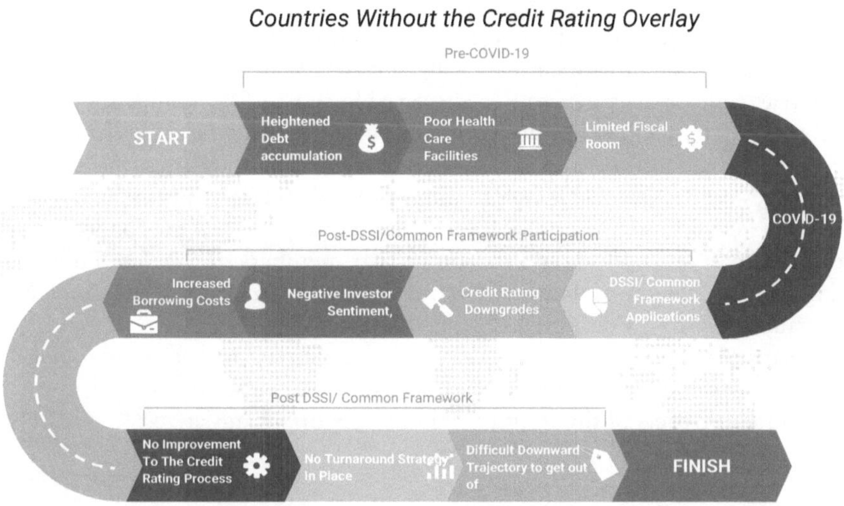

Figure 4.1 Countries Without the Credit Rating Overlay

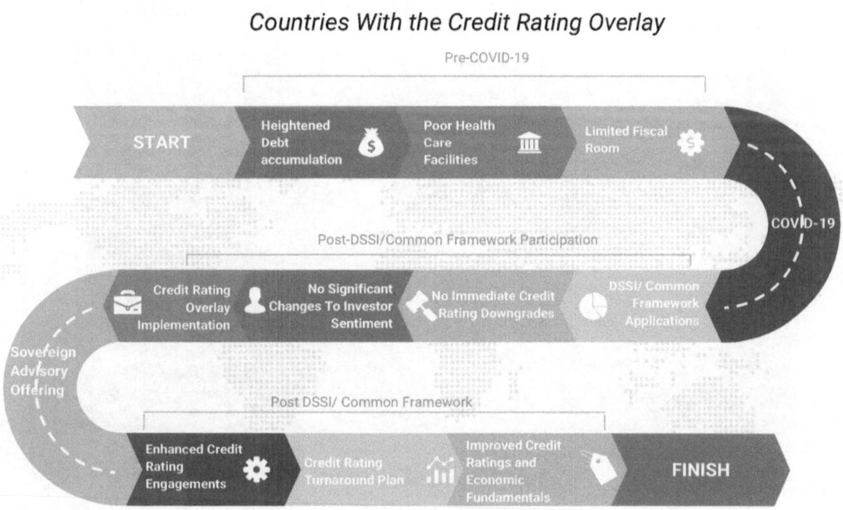

Figure 4.2 Countries With the Credit Rating Overlay

sovereign's creditworthiness. Fitch said that 'as Fitch recognises that no quantitative model can fully capture all the relevant influences on sovereign creditworthiness, the agency also employs a QO designed to adjust for factors that are not reflected or not fully reflected in the SRM (Sovereign Rating Master [criteria]) for any individual rating'. The key to the idea of an overlay is that 'the QO is used to provide a subjective assessment, consistent with criteria, *of key factors within these rating criteria that are not able to be fully incorporated or reflected in the SRM*'.[15] Fitch's overlay stands to increase or decrease certain ratings *within* the rating process for a sovereign and is forward-looking: 'The QO is predominantly forward-looking in nature, based partly on Fitch's economic and financial projections, thereby complementing the SRM, which includes a mix of historical and forward-looking data (one year of forecasts as part of three-year centred averages for certain variables). The QO comprises a rating adjustment system applied to the SRM output, with a potential notching range of +2/−2 for each of the four analytical pillars (structural features, macro, public finances, and external finances) and an overall rating adjustment range of +3/−3 for each rating, except in certain circumstances'.[16] This concept of an overlay then is not radical, and the other two members of the Big Three use similar approaches across a range of rating sectors, ranging from municipalities to sustainability-based ratings.[17]

In terms of how a multilateral initiative-based overlay may work, Figure 4.3[18] illustrates what elements could be considered by the rating overlay to promote the ideals and targets of the multilateral debt treatment initiative.

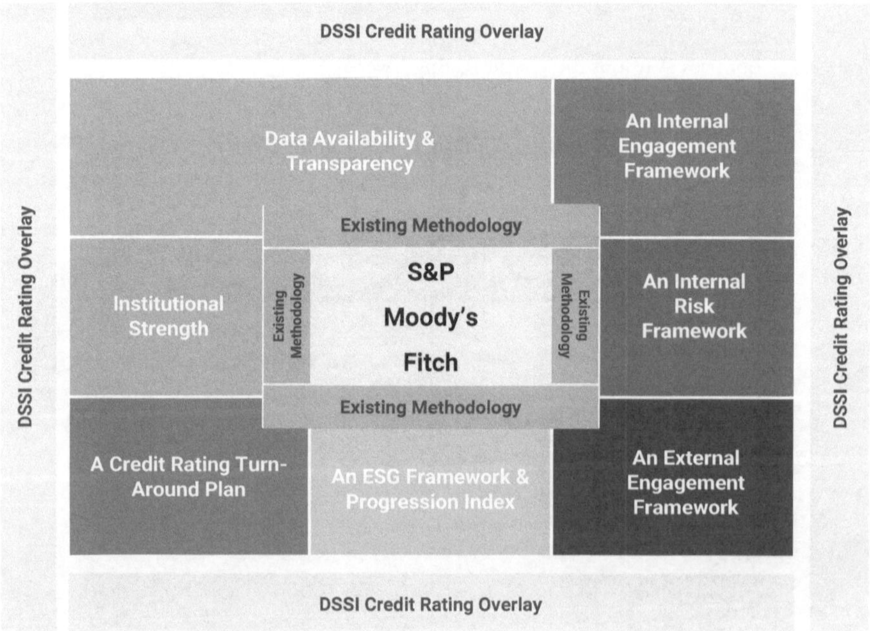

Figure 4.3 DSSI Credit Rating Overlay

Remembering that the third component to this stage of the solution is advisory services serving sovereigns to better build and implement internal processes, you can see here that the proposed rating overlay would *reward* instances of successful implementation. Whilst some of the elements illustrated above may be considered to be extra to what is usually required from a multilateral debt treatment initiative (think 'structural adjustment', which is often economic in nature), the ability to build into the solution elements of ESG and climate change progression can be a key benefit of the solution, both for the debtors and creditors, as well as for the global picture. The idea would be to have pre-agreed targets for vulnerable countries in each of these categories, which would be proportionate to the situation the vulnerable countries find themselves in, that is, setting targets for vulnerable countries to be world-leading in the space of a year is not appropriate. However, as the pre-agreed targets would be proportionate, the penalty for not meeting those targets would be that the temporary rating overlay would become null-and-void, with the sovereign then being exposed to the potential of being rated as being in default. Figure 4.4[19] illustrates the details of each of the categories.

In Figure 4.4, you can see that the variables are split into two sides – four on one side and three on the other. This is to differentiate them between 'high impact outcomes' and 'process enhancers'. The process enhancers, if pre-agreed targets are achieved, would serve to provide a foundation for achievements in the other categories. The high-impact outcomes, if pre-agreed targets are achieved, would serve to translate into credit enhancements (notches) over the medium- to long-term. There is potential via this solution, therefore, to come out of it in a much better position in terms of a sovereign's creditworthiness. In addition, it injects, incorporates, and almost institutionalises a long-term foundation upon which the sovereigns can grow as opposed to remaining in the debt cycle. Figure 4.5[20] details how this separation of the different elements would affect the rating overlay process.

The process would involve quarterly reviews based on a yearly framework. Because of the process effectively side-stepping the crucial process whereby credit rating agencies warn investors of potential losses, the proposed resolution must be strict. The implementation of so many reviews as to how countries are progressing with their side of the bargain is crucial if private entities are to allow the resolution to be implemented. Thus, it is a necessary trade-off. In terms of how the countries may exit the solution, there are several options. The country may simply move back to the normal rating scale after the 12-month period, but hopefully in a much healthier position than when it entered; it would have implemented key fundamentals (at least at the very early stages of a long-term implementation) and would have had the chance to restructure its finances within the 12 months offered. For those where 12 months is not long enough to restructure their debts, applications could be made to the multilateral institutions in charge of the debt treatment initiative to which the solution is attached, for an extension based on particular circumstances. Signatories to the solution (credit rating agencies and private creditors) would have accepted

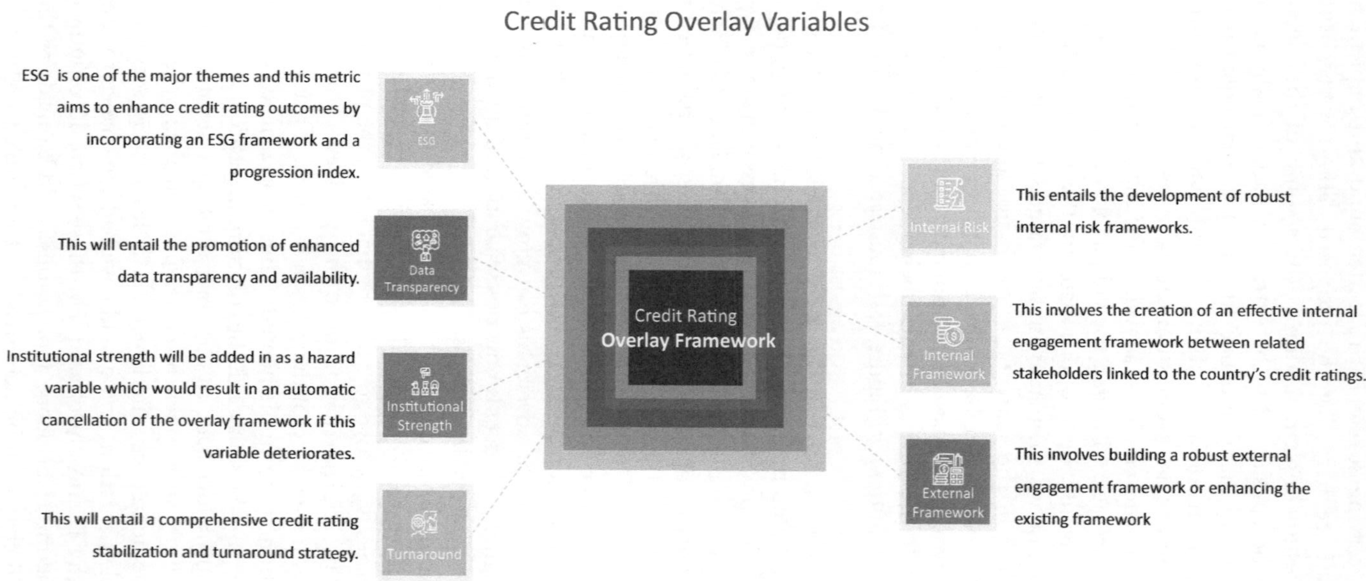

Figure 4.4 Credit Rating Overlay Framework

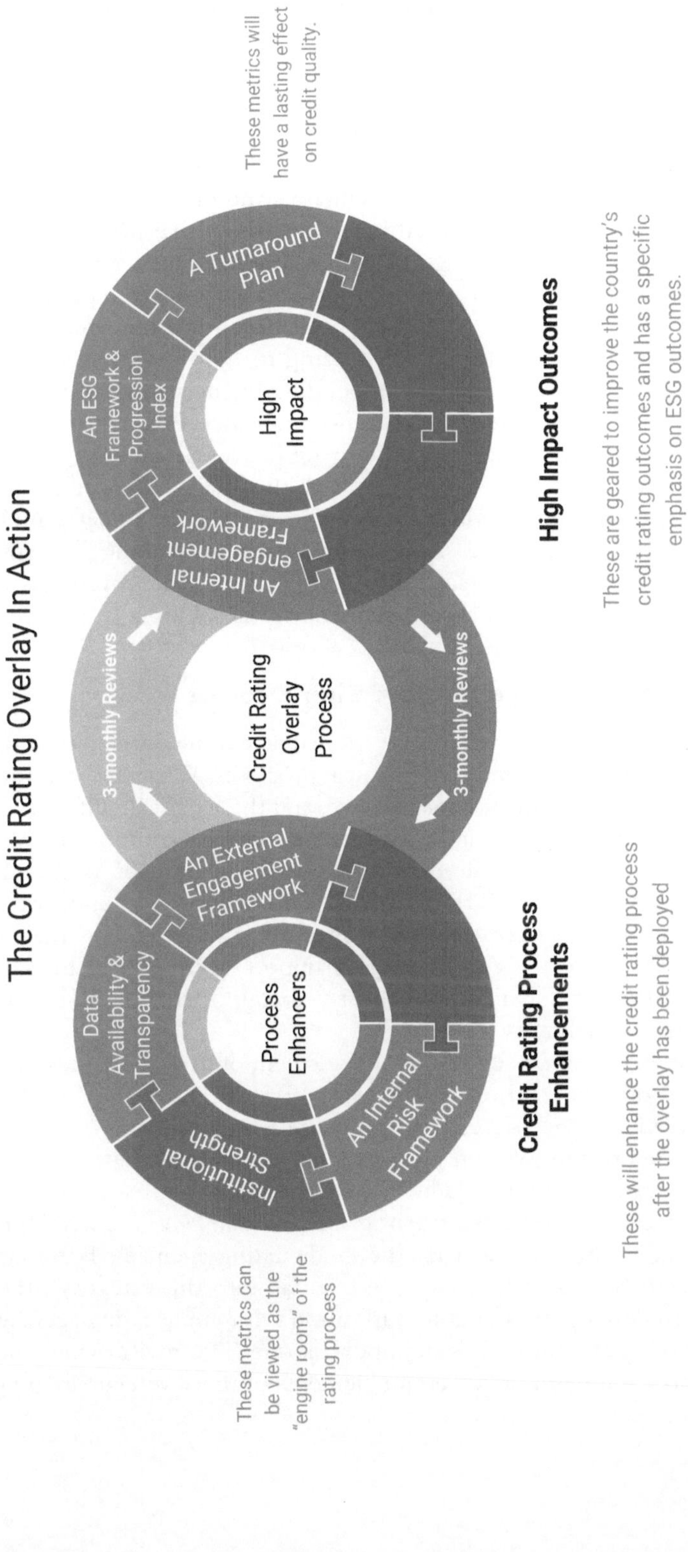

Figure 4.5 Credit Rating Overlay in Action

this condition at the beginning of the implementation, although there would need to be an agreed-upon maximum length of time the solution could be applied.

It is clear that the development of a *collaborative* environment within the sovereign debt sector is required to do something like that being proposed here. That has been sorely lacking, but the idea is that the solution provides incentives for all parties. Credit rating agencies can continue their role, but that role becomes much more socially facilitative and provides the credit rating agencies with positive regard, something which they have not received for a long time. The private creditors get to restructure their loan agreements with a longer vision in mind, which can mean more returns over the period (rather than threatened returns as is currently the situation, in that the countries could default at any moment) whilst also continuing to have the protection of the credit rating process to warn them of impending financial stress in the debtors (being taken out of the solution for non-compliance or underperformance would place the sovereign back into the firing line of the rating agencies and the default ratings). Lastly, the sovereigns have the space and impetus to build much stronger fundamentals which have the potential to be *lasting*, with better relationships with creditors and credit rating agencies providing for a stronger base upon which they can develop. This is why assisting the sovereigns with a sovereign advisory service is a crucial element of the solution.

4.4 An Advisory Service for Sovereign Debtors

Several private endeavours are being developed across the developing world to assist a sovereign with their internal financial processes. What this solution calls for is a credit rating-specific advisory service, and these exist in different forms. There is potential for a small industry to be developed around this solution, with different regions across the developing world in need of local resources that can aid their sovereigns' development. This proposed solution does not seek to dictate what that service would offer but offers elements that would be important for the sovereign. In terms of support, there is space here for the connected civil society organisations to play an important role in supporting the development of advisory services.

Every sovereign would need an initial assessment of their fundamentals. This would allow both the advisor and the sovereign to better understand their short-term needs and then develop a plan to attain their medium- to long-term goals. If attached to the solution presented here, getting processes in place to meet the quarterly reviews would be crucial. Amongst the first steps would be to ensure that the right processes are in place to *communicate* the developments to the required entities, particularly the credit rating agencies. For countries that are unrated (several vulnerable countries fall into this category), the first step may be to develop lines of communication with credit rating agencies.

This issue of communication is an important one. The advisor would be able to devise a plan and ensure that certain elements of the sovereign are prepared for what is required of them. Certain ministries within the sovereign may be better placed to liaise with the credit rating agencies pre-emptively and, therefore, provide richer information for the credit rating process. This would need to be part of the earliest plans of the advisor. However, there may need to be a shake-up of the internal structure, with the potential of the creation of new internal departments, to even liaise with the sovereign advisor so that the process can be as efficient as possible (as it would need to be to meet the demands of the solution).

As part of the solution, the country will need access to software options. Software exists that monitors and interprets the credit rating agencies' methodologies and, as a result, can closely predict a sovereign credit rating based upon the inputs of the sovereign. This would be crucial to the establishment of an effective plan of action for the sovereign so that it knows the exact areas of its position that need to be worked on more than others to meet particular targets. Creating adapted software options for the solution, if it were to be implemented, would not be difficult and would feed into the programme of pre-emptive design for the sovereign's internal aspects.

The advisory service element of the solution, as hinted at in the description of what it would entail above, relies heavily on the sovereign engaging with the process. Sharing vital information in a transparent manner is the only way the process can work. Several research investigations have found a bias in credit ratings towards developed countries, so it is not surprising that there is a lack of trust. The solution would aim to resolve this by employing intermediaries, in the shape of locally developed advisory services, that can seek to cut through any issues that may lead to the development of biases on the sovereign side (a lack of transparency or a lack of internal governance, for example). This could be revolutionary for the sovereigns because as they are learning, if one wants to engage with the capital markets, then they *have* to engage with the gatekeepers as well, and that gatekeeper has particular dynamics which cannot be ignored. With the implementation of an advisory service that specialises in credit rating research, some of the asymmetry that exists can be lessened to cultivate a much better relationship moving forward. The harsh truth is that if a developing sovereign wants to turn into a developed sovereign, they will need to positively engage with the credit rating process – there is no other way in the system as it exists today.

4.5 Conclusion

This solution, as presented in this chapter, has potential. It is without precedent, but that does not mean much when we consider that other elements in the field once started without precedent. It requires a shift in mentality, but not a fundamental one. Whilst collaboration is key for the solution to work, the solution has within it incentives to appeal to the self-interest of all the parties. This is important because for the majority of debt treatment initiatives, somebody has to lose. For a long-term effect to be realised, the concept of 'loss' needs to be removed as much as possible.

The solution is the first part of a two-stage plan, and it is clear to see why. The solution will not be picked up voluntarily because it would exist on a legal footing that was not designed for its implementation. The exposure to liability for the credit rating agencies, at the moment, is far too great. This is why the next stage of the two-stage plan, presented in the next chapter, is to consider *all* of the legislation and regulation that affects credit rating agencies when it comes to their methodologies and processes and, crucially, the inflexibility that surrounds those elements. It is not difficult to see why there is legislative and regulatory inflexibility surrounding the rating agencies and their methodological processes because at the core of almost all of their transgressions over the past two decades, alterations to their methodologies for financial gain have proven to be the most problematic. The EU has perhaps been the most vociferous in its legislating against the credit rating agencies in this respect, and it is clear why; the EU was badly affected by the sovereign ratings of the credit rating agencies during the Eurozone debt crisis in the early 2010s, and it regulated accordingly afterwards (on top of the fact that they had no legislative history with the credit rating agencies). To 'over-regulate' in that regard makes perfect sense. However, now there needs to be a re-assessment of that legislative approach across the major legislative centres because the world has changed. That inflexibility is now causing real harm. Yet, deregulation is not the answer. Deregulating the credit rating industry could have catastrophic consequences solely because the constitution of the credit rating industry cannot be trusted; it has proven this on several occasions. The 'stickiness' of the credit rating industry and its utility despite underperformance mean that transgressions for financial gain are a constant threat facing legislators and regulators. This is why this project calls for 're-regulation', which is very different. The reduction in inflexibility in this *specific* sector and for a very *temporary* period is required to break the credit rating impasse, and this will be presented in the next chapter, and subsequently campaigned for with the help of supportive individuals and organisations that also seek to overcome the credit rating impasse.

Leaving aside those legal concerns for a moment, the plan proposed in this chapter has very different aims from a lot of the proposals being put forward in the field at the moment. Not to compare and critique, but they are different in constitution. For example, the call for countries to default and return is short-term and ignores the long-term consequences. This proposal aims to put a plan in place that can transcend the COVID-19 pandemic and become a model for future crises. The wish, of course, is that countries will be better prepared for future economic crises because of the implementation of the solution, but that would be naïve. The model of alleviating the pressure on sovereign debtors at times of crisis, considering the ever-growing importance of the capital markets, could be an important addition to the sovereign debt marketplace that does not have an internationally agreed upon bankruptcy procedure in place. It strongly appears that there is no political force strong enough to impose a bankruptcy procedure on the global marketplace for sovereign debt; as such, a temporary mechanism could resolve the systemic threat of mass defaults (although it would not aid single aspects of financial stress).

For this to take place, there needs to be movement on all sides, and therein lies the difficulty in this proposal. Campaigning, therefore, is key to pushing for change and consideration of a change in certain roles within the financial architecture. In that regard, and with regards to other endeavours that are designed, entities such as civil society, academics, and relevant media outlets will be crucial in helping to alleviate the pressure on the world's most vulnerable now and in the future.

Notes

1 The Credit Rating Research Initiative, *Developing a Credit Rating Solution for the World's Poorest Countries: An African Focus* (2021) www.aston.ac.uk/sites/default/files/Policy%20Proposal%20with%20Amendments.pdf.
2 For an example of the range of issues raised regarding the developing world and climate change, see Anil Markandya and Kirsten Halsnaes (eds), *Climate Change and Sustainable Development: Prospects for Developing Countries* (Routledge 2021).
3 Institute of International Finance, *Principles for Stable Capital Flows and Fair Debt Restructuring: Report on Implementation by the Principles Consultative Group* (2020) www.iif.com/Portals/0/Files/content/Regulatory/10_23_2020_pcg_report_2020.pdf 6.
4 IOSCO, *The Role of Credit Rating Agencies in Structured Finance Markets* (2008) www.iosco.org/library/pubdocs/pdf/IOSCOPD263.pdf.
5 Ibid 13.
6 ACT, *Comments in Response to Consultation Report: The Role of Credit Rating Agencies in Structured Finance Markets* (2008) www.treasurers.org/ACTmedia/ACTRespStrtdratings0308.pdf.
7 SEC, *Report to Congress: Credit Rating Standardization Study* (2012) www.sec.gov/files/939h_credit_rating_standardization.pdf.
8 Ibid.
9 Regulation (EC) No 1060/2009 10.3.
10 Tracy Alloway, '(sf) Stands for Structured Finance' (2010) *Financial Times* (Mar 16) www.ft.com/content/bf269488-c554-334c-8a2d-af915531c6fe.
11 Tracy Alloway, 'Symbolic Structured Finance' (2010) *Financial Times* (Feb 16) www.ft.com/content/d727db08-49f4-3b92-b6eb-23373b1c5779.
12 SEC (n 7) KBRA adopted the additional identifier, see page 51.
13 Figures 4.1 and 4.2 are taken from: The Credit Rating Research Initiative (n 1) 33.
14 Bogie Ozdemir and Peter Miu, *Basel II Implementation: A Guide to Developing and Validating a Complaint, Internal Risk Rating System* (McGraw-Hill Professional 2008) 10.
15 Fitch Ratings, 'Sovereign Rating Criteria: Master Criteria' (2020) *Fitch Ratings* (Oct 26) www.fitchratings.com/research/sovereigns/sovereign-rating-criteria-26-10-2020 7 (emphasis added).
16 Ibid.
17 For example, see S&P's Quantitative Government Support Overlay (S&P Global), 'Quantitative Government Support Overlay for Local Government Financing Vehicles (LGFVs) 1.0' (2021) *S&P Global* (Oct 20) www.spglobal.com/marketintelligence/en/news-insights/research/quantitative-government-support-overlay-for-local-government-financing-vehicles-lgfvs-1) and Moody's RiskCalc Qualitative Overlay, described here at Moody's, 'RiskCalc Qualitative Overlay' (2016) www.moodysanalytics.com/-/media/products/RiskCalc-Qualitative-Overlay-Factsheet.pdf.
18 The Credit Rating Research Initiative (n 1) 12.
19 Ibid 13.
20 Ibid 14.

5 Resolving the Credit Rating Impasse

Part Two

5.1 Introduction

In the previous chapter, the first stage of the book's proposal to develop reform that can break the credit rating impasse was presented. However, underlying all of that chapter was the understanding that whilst encouraging certain players into the plan may be beneficial, something much more formal must be added to the equation. To allow for the credit rating agencies to do what the book is asking, there needs to be legislative reform to allow them to do it. The targeted and temporary reduction in potential liability for the credit rating agencies is not only important but is technically *required* if the credit rating agencies are to do anything differently. We have identified so far in the book that if the situation stays as it is, the credit rating impasse will persist in blocking countries from renegotiating their private debt holdings; nothing yet has been proposed that will allow each of the players to continue serving their own interests, whilst simultaneously serving the needs of others until now.

I have made this point clear before but will do so again; what is being proposed here is not *de*regulation but rather *re*regulation, and that is very different. We shall see in this chapter that the legislators across the dominant credit rating markets reacted to the Financial Crisis in different ways, but formally building a regulatory framework to adequately surround the credit rating agencies and their ratings was given the utmost priority. In a lot of the sections of those frameworks, the coverage was more than adequate and has succeeded in curtailing particular practices that were fundamental components of the credit rating agencies' transgressive behaviour. In other areas, attempts to undertake certain legislative endeavours, such as increasing competition within the sector, have proven to be difficult to implement in reality. In other sectors, regulators have found that it is more beneficial to the running of the financial system to almost disregard elements of the legislative endeavours that were developed. However, a theme that underlies the majority of the actions taken after the Financial Crisis is that the frameworks were supposed to hold the agencies to account more than ever before.

If we add to this formal legislative/regulatory endeavour the settlements between S&P and Moody's and the US Department of Justice, it becomes clear

DOI: 10.4324/9781003261223-6

that the concept of the agencies being held liable for their actions was brought to the fore in a major way. Though I have shown before that the development of the unnecessary ancillary service divisions of the agencies essentially protected the agencies from those record financial penalties,[1] the effect of reminding the agencies that liability needs to be considered at all times was an important development (though I argue that they never forgot this but merely understood that the potential liability costs were outweighed by the bounty of the subprime mortgage racket). Since the Financial Crisis, the agencies have been consistently reminding the market that their ratings are opinions and should not be relied upon and that whilst the new regulations have pushed them to be more transparent, it is they who will decide on how to formulate a credit rating and it is not the place of the State to enforce any sort of standard, which is stance regulators and legislators have had to accept. However, when we look at the post-Financial Crisis regulations, it becomes clear that some inflexibility has developed as a by-product of the need to protect society from the inequity of the credit rating arena. In the shape of sovereign ratings, we have a perfect example of that inflexibility. Post-Financial Crisis regulations dictated that credit rating agencies needed to publish their methodological processes and stick to them, with the vast majority of the financial penalties apportioned by regulators to rating agencies since the Financial Crisis because the agencies said one thing and did another. Now, the credit rating agencies are saying that they cannot do anything but that which they are doing with sovereign ratings because their published methodologies determine their scope of analysis. This book argues that this needs to change in *specific circumstances*; reregulation, not deregulation.

5.2 A New Legal World for Credit Rating Agencies

In the mid-2000s, the environment around the credit rating agencies began to change dramatically. The regulatory freedom that the agencies enjoyed, to the point of having regulation consolidate their oligopolistic industry, was under intense scrutiny, and the two major centres for credit rating regulation – the US and the EU – were beginning to, in their own unique ways, chart particular regulatory courses that would change the regulatory environment for the agencies forever.

However, in this section, we highlight several caveats before we continue. It is not within the scope of this book to present a detailed history of the legal developments within the two jurisdictions because, quite simply, there have been other scholarly endeavours that have provided near-perfect accounts, and which should be read to gain a detailed understanding of the legal developments surrounding the credit rating agencies.[2] There are, however, elements of that building of a regulatory framework on either side of the Atlantic Ocean which provide key themes, which will aid with understanding the potential for a nuanced redrawing of particular elements of the credit rating regulatory sphere. As a final caveat, the reason for selecting the jurisdictions of the US and EU is that the US is the home of the credit rating agencies; the EU has, in many ways, taken the lead in regulating key aspects of the credit rating agencies' world; and the majority of other jurisdictions around the world either model themselves on the US Securities and Exchange Commission or have entered into memorandums of understanding and equivalence with their European counterparts.

There are key differences in how the US and the EU have chosen to regulate the credit rating agencies, and those differences stem from the sets of circumstances that applied to those jurisdictions at particular times (and which forced the regulations) and from the traditions of the two regions which are markedly different. In the US, the regulation of the credit rating agencies was, up until 2005/6, non-existent. The agencies were regulated, in a way, by the SEC via the concept of an agency being a Nationally Recognised Statistical Rating Organisation (NRSRO), which was developed in 1975 (but promulgated in 1973). This was done using Rule 15c3–1, also known as the 'Net Capital Rule', which was 'essentially designed to ensure "that registered broker-dealers have adequate liquid assets to meet their obligations to their investors and creditors"'.[3] This development came at the same time that credit rating agencies began charging issuers to develop ratings rather than subscribers. The rules established in 1973 had the effect of consolidating the rating agencies' position within the marketplace by inserting their ratings into key regulatory areas as a method of measuring and verifying creditworthiness. However, the process for being designated as an NRSRO was opaque and was developed without any formal standards but merely relied upon 'market acceptance of rating agencies in designating NRSROs'.[4] I have written elsewhere about the reliance upon 'market acceptance' during that era, with the classic example being that there is a theory within the literature that suggests credit rating agencies were miraculously saved by the SEC with the 1973 rule as they were almost going out of business; this does not make sense (why would the SEC save a dying industry like this and catapult them into a guaranteed oligopoly?), but the reality does, in that there was a competitor (the National Credit Office) who had dominated the market by giving out massively inflated ratings before the collapse of the Penn Central Railroad in 1970. The collapse of the railroad left investors with massive losses, and it shook the trust in the National Credit Office; the rating agencies offered a different approach (in theory) that the market flocked to, and the SEC merely followed suit with its 1973 regulation that encapsulated the market's move.[5] The point here is that the US has always been keen on allowing the market to take the lead in defining best practices, particularly in the field of credit ratings.

For decades afterwards, the credit rating industry slowly but surely became more important within the American financial fabric. As the largest agencies manoeuvred themselves via IPOs (Moody's) and internal reorganisations between parent companies (S&P and Fitch), the world around them was hurtling towards the 2000s, an era within which the concepts of 'structured finance' and 'asset securitisation' would become forever connected. Despite the era of hubris, there were murmurings regarding the role and importance of credit rating agencies, and in 2006, the US enacted its first-ever piece of legislation aimed at the credit rating agencies. The new Act was developed in relation to a proposal the SEC put forward which set out the definition and constraints for NRSRO. After enacting a smaller and somewhat of a gateway piece of legislation in 2005 (The Credit Rating Agency Duopoly Relief Act), the more substantial Credit Rating Agency Reform Act 2006 was enacted, which provided the SEC with the statutory authority to implement rules regarding the registration, record-keeping, financial reporting, and oversight of the CRAs.[6] However, as Miglionico discusses, the Act did not give the SEC the licence to intervene in the ratings and methodologies themselves, with the Act confirming clearly that 'notwithstanding any other provision of law, neither the Commission nor any State or political subdivision thereof may regulate the substance of credit ratings or the procedures and methodologies by which any nationally recognised statistical rating organisation determines credit ratings'.[7] This was done for two reasons. First, there is a long-held theory, which the credit rating agencies themselves are the biggest champions of, that says the usefulness and role of the agencies depend, absolutely, on their *independence* which any regulatory intervention would obviously damage. Second, the market, the rights of the private business entity (and this transcends into public corporations oddly), and the freedom to opinion are fundamental and constituent parts of the American culture. However, the Act did enforce increased transparency for the agencies, with the Act dictating that particular performance measures needed to be made public by the CRAs so that their performance could be better judged by industry users.[8]

Nevertheless, it was too little too late. Despite the 2006 Act containing several rules regarding structured finance and its rating of it, the horse had long since left the stable (in fact, it had left the farm entirely). The Financial Crisis of 2007 and 2008 brought the US (and others, of course) to its knees, and the credit rating agencies were immediately found to be central characters (or villains) in the debacle. As the 2006 Act was mainly concerned with formalising the registration of already-cemented agencies (it, coincidentally, had very little effect on promoting competition; some claim that it, in reality, hindered it by allowing the leading agencies to influence the design of the rulings that the SEC were trusted with designing on the back of Act),[9] it was decided that there needed to be new legislation just four years later, and that was done by including a credit rating-specific section in the Financial Crisis-related Dodd–Frank Wall Street Reform and Consumer Protection Act of 2010. Sections 931–939H were dedicated to the rating agencies and sought to affect different aspects of their business, ranging from enhancing the transparency of rating processes and removing the references to ratings within regulations, to enforcing qualification standards for rating analysts, considering universal credit ratings (which did not happen), and (for the first time) allowing for investors to file civil suits against credit rating agencies for the content of their ratings.

There were limited provisions within the Act that allowed for private civil action to be pursued; however, although it was limited, it was crucial in the record settlements that followed the Financial Crisis in 2015 and 2017 with S&P and Moody's, respectively. Yet, whilst that case, which was initiated by CalPERS and saw Fitch allegedly provide information to aid with the case as part of its own settlement with CalPERS (which CalPERS needed to satisfy the standards dictated in the Act), represents the pinnacle of action taken against the Big Two agencies, the overarching reality was that the aim to open agencies up to liability was to lead the SEC into a place it simply did not want to be. Miglionico states:

> Regarding liability, the Dodd-Frank Act creates a new regime in which issuers have to obtain permission from NRSROs to use their ratings in their prospectuses and NRSROs are subject to the same standards as public accountants and securities analysts. NRSROs are liable as experts under the Securities Act of 1933 when they consent to the disclosure of their ratings in a prospectus. This means that rating agencies are no longer exempt of First Amendment defences from private right of action.[10]

This put the rating agencies in a corner. Prior to the enactment of the Dodd–Frank Act, the exposure to liability that credit rating agencies faced when having their ratings included in prospectus' was taken away by Rule 436(g) of the Securities Act of 1933. The Dodd–Frank Act repealed that rule and exposed the agencies to liability as experts under Section 11 of the Securities Act, with the sentiment being that such central gatekeepers should be held accountable. However, the agencies have always maintained that their ratings are merely 'opinions' and that, as such, they are protected by the constitutional right to free speech. For an issuance to be taken to market *with* a credit rating attached (and which, in reality, is necessary for a number of reasons), the issuer must obtain the consent of the credit rating agency to do so. In retaliation to the Dodd–Frank Act, the credit rating agencies responded that they would not be giving consent for their ratings to be used. As Carbone notes, 'perhaps unwittingly, with the stroke of a pen, President Obama single-handedly shut down the new offerings market for both investment-grade debt and asset-backed securities on July 22 and left public companies unable to raise capital in offerings registered under the Securities Act'.[11] Leaving aside the issue that this development should have been predicted by lawmakers, the credit rating agencies had played their 'joker', and it worked perfectly. In response to the projected seizure of the financial marketplace, the SEC quickly acted. On the same day as the repeal of Rule 436(g) became effective, the SEC issued a 'no-action letter' to Ford Motor Credit Company LLC because a $1 billion auto-ABS issuance could not go through without the inclusion of a credit rating in its prospectus. Ford requested that items 1103(a)(9) and 1120 of 'Regulation AB' that mandated a prospectus must include a credit rating be overlooked and that enforcement would not be forthcoming if Ford was to issue a debt package *without* a credit rating attached; the SEC's 'no-action' letter, that is, no action will be taken, duly obliged and had the effect of overriding the aim of exposing the credit rating agencies to expert liability under Section 11 of the Securities Act, and it has been that way ever since.[12]

Whilst the credit rating agencies did indeed play their ace card, the other outcome was a clear message to those interested in the regulation of the credit rating agencies in the US: the market must come first. What works for the marketplace will be maintained even if it means circumventing the will of Congress and the President. This is because the functioning markets are central to the US economy as they are to all economies, but 'successful market' is a concept that is engrained within the American culture and will be given priority at all times. This is not to say that this approach is right or wrong, but it helps us when we want to consider what regulatory reforms may be possible and how to frame them. We will be doing that in the next section, but on the other side of the Atlantic Ocean, credit rating reform was taking a very different path.

The EU, by its constitution at the very least, will always have a very different relationship with the credit rating agencies than the US has. Leaving aside that the leading agencies are all American entities, the multi-sovereign-state constitution of the EU means that the credit rating agencies can have a much more contagious impact on the health of the Union than it can in the US. The EU is also more vulnerable to the wider marketplace than the more established and more globally integrated the US is. These factors play a role in how the EU see the rating agencies.

The analyses and murmurings that led to the Credit Rating Agency Reform Act of 2006 in the US were present in the EU as well. With some of the major European banks being exposed to the US subprime market, questions were being raised as to whether the EU understood the role and potential impact of the credit rating agencies well. In early 2004, the EU adopted a resolution that put forward its position on the credit rating agencies after investigation, a resolution which confirmed that it both understood the potential positives of the credit rating agencies and their impact on the credit markets, but that there were also 'problematic issues' which were present that potentially warranted further action. It put forward the idea of developing a registration system for credit rating agencies operating in the EU, akin to the NRSRO designation system, and it proposed that by 31st July 2005, the European Commission should present its assessment of whether legislative proposals were needed to deal with the identified problematic issues.

Today, developed as a post-Financial Crisis response, we have the European Securities and Markets Authority (ESMA), but its predecessor was the Committee of European Securities Regulators (CESR), and it was to the CESR that the European Commission turned for assistance. The European Commission asked the CESR for its views on whether formal regulation was required, and the CESR responded that it was not.[13] The CESR instead opted for a system based on self-regulation, whereby the aim was to monitor the agencies and how well they complied with the voluntary rules set out by the International Organisation of Securities Commissions (IOSCO), which sit as an umbrella organisation of the world's securities regulators and attempt to dictate industry norms across industries via an array of soft law instruments. The viewpoint was that existing financial directives adopted by the EU would be more than adequate as they applied to credit rating agencies. The CESR's subsequent investigations into the rating agencies found that they were broadly compliant with the IOSCO codes (themselves developed in conjunction with agencies), apart from in the areas of unsolicited ratings and ancillary services.

Arguably, the European regulators had not fully understood those they were regulating, or worst, still trusted them too much. Either way, Europe was left defenceless against the rating agencies and the actions they were taking, although the enactment of the 2006 Act in the US did not protect the Americans either. The Financial Crisis was to rip through the EU just like it did the US, and as a result, the decision was taken to change course and formally legislate against the rating agencies for the first time.

The first piece of formal legislation came in 2009, with 'Regulation No 1060/2009'. This piece of legislation essentially sought to target the issues of the internal conflicts of interest within the rating industry and the quality of the ratings. It incorporated several market terminologies and practices into the formal legislative sphere, with some suggesting that it was 'well balanced'.[14] However, others argued that it had failed in many aspects, mainly because it did not adequately address several important issues, including rating competency, methodologies, disclosure, and accountability.[15] Operationally, the legislation empowered the relevant 'competent national authorities' (selected financial regulators in each Member State) to regulate the agencies, but this was problematic. To resolve this and other systemic issues, the EU decided to upgrade its regulatory architecture and, in 2011, it formed the European Securities and Markets Authority (ESMA), which is a Union-wide regulator in several fields, and it was deemed important that credit rating regulation in the Union became centralised. Thus, in 2011, the EU implemented its second piece of CRA-related legislation, 'Regulation No 513/2011' or CRA Regulation II. This legislation empowered ESMA to coordinate the competent national authorities and develop a registration system, whereby any credit rating agency wishing to ply its trade in the EU would need to register with ESMA, and in doing so open itself up to scrutiny by the new regulator. The increase in obligation was significant, and ESMA immediately began with its on-site checks, reporting, and feedback mechanisms.[16]

Yet, the mistake made by regulators in the mid-2000s in not legislating for the credit rating agencies sooner was to come to bear. In 2011, as the EU consolidated its regulation of the agencies, the impact of credit ratings and the contagion they can cause was to dramatically affect the EU, even threatening its survival as a bloc. As I mentioned earlier, the EU and the US have fundamentally different relationships with the credit rating agencies because of their constitution (as well as the leading agencies being American). As Lane discusses in relation to the Sovereign Debt Crisis of 2011:

> The capacity of the euro-member countries to withstand negative macroeconomic and financial shocks was identified as a major challenge for the success of the euro from the beginning. By switching off the option for national currency devaluations, a traditional adjustment mechanism between national economies was eliminated. Moreover, the euro area did not match the design of the 'dollar union' of the United States in key respects, since the monetary union was not accompanied by a significant degree of banking union or fiscal union. Rather, it was deemed feasible to retain national responsibility for financial regulation and fiscal policy.[17]

This desire to maintain national responsibility comes from the underlying foundations of the Union and the need to respect national heritage and sovereignty in what is not the strongest of Unions – remember, it is not the *United* States of Europe. Nevertheless, the effects of the Financial Crisis and the slowing of investment flows left many weaker EU Member States vulnerable, and many countries needed substantial assistance and support (e.g. Greece, Portugal, Spain, and Ireland). As a result, but in a very procyclical manner, the credit rating agencies downgraded the sovereign ratings of numerous countries in the Eurozone *en masse*. This, as some have observed, was not a new phenomenon; Gaillard rightly notes that 'the inability of credit rating agencies to anticipate sovereign debt-crises and the tendency to overreact once financial difficulties have piled up are well-known phenomena'.[18] Several excellent works have examined the debt crisis that engulfed the EU in 2011 and onwards,[19] but essentially, the key element for us is that the credit rating agencies were extraordinarily late to the party and then made things significantly worse when they arrived. As a result, the EU decided in 2013 to legislate for the credit rating agencies again.

Regulation No 462/2013 had a number of aims, including more transparency regarding procedural elements within agencies; tellingly, it also aimed to review 'the timing of publication specifically for sovereign ratings'. In the US and in the Dodd–Frank Act, there are no specific provisions relating to sovereign debt ratings,[20] which is not surprising, given the lack of effect that sovereign ratings have upon the American experience. However, now that the EU was under bombardment by sovereign credit ratings, the concept became central to the legislative effort. The issue was mentioned more than 50 times in the legislation, and the focus was on transparency at all levels of developing a sovereign rating and then in the timeliness of publishing them. Yet, the EU refused to intervene in the methodologies themselves, which exemplifies the sanctity of the private right to conduct business.

Ultimately, the debt crisis was a 'wake-up' call for the EU, and even at the point of writing, the Union is still feeling the effects of the rating bombardment (Greece is yet to return to 'investment-grade', though it is apparently close). The mistakes of the mid-2000s were not repeated, and the EU now stands at the forefront of CRA regulation, mostly because it has to; its composition and structure demand protection from the rating agencies. The two different approaches, particularly when it comes to sovereign ratings, have changed the landscape for credit rating agencies. They are now under much more scrutiny, and despite the regulatory inability to impose liability (for reasons we have discussed), the credit rating agencies have taken the new architecture seriously. This is not to say that the larger agencies have not transgressed since the Financial Crisis; they have (with several fines, settlements, and even suspensions from rating certain areas of the financial sector being given), but now the agencies are making clear that compliance is a key concern for their business. It is this dynamic that lies at the heart of the credit rating impasse and now we know why we can finally move forward with how to resolve it.

5.3 Areas for Reform

It is not the intention of this book to write new legislation. It is also not the intention of the book to tell legislators what the new legislation would look like for the plan it is proposing to be established. This is because the legislation that exists would need to be amended in a particular way so as not to infringe upon other legal facets of the legislative sphere. It is also important for the credit rating agencies to have their say so that the legislative amendments that the book suggests are needed are practicable. There are many vitally important caveats to state before we continue.

The first is that this needs to be a collaborative process. Imposing these changes upon the credit rating agencies and the capital markets will not work; there are far too many 'jokers' that can be played to stifle the development needed, and those 'jokers' will be played if any of the participants feel that their position is being threatened or weakened (like we saw in the aftermath of the Dodd–Frank Act). This is rational. The second caveat is that this proposal is based on relative ease for all concerned to increase the chances of its success. For that reason, it is suggested here that a new piece of legislation is not necessarily required and that small amendments could be made (potentially by way of statutory instruments that *insert* rather than fundamentally alter). For these reasons, this section will highlight the sections of the relevant legislation that would need to be considered for amendment, should the proposal be implemented.

However, before that, I want to make the proposal clear in as succinct a way as possible. The plan is for the credit rating agencies to develop a temporary and focused 'overlay' that encourages all of the elements that the DSSI and Common Framework seek to encourage, alongside climate and ESG-related developments. This overlay becomes applicable only when a country enters those (and any future) multilateral-designed debt treatment programmes and remains in place for the duration. The overlay will have a credit rating symbol system attached to it which, at once, declares to investors the country's financial health in relation to the indicators set out by the multilateral programme and the rating agencies and (crucially) allows the country to stave off the dreaded default grade that fundamentally kills its chances to renegotiate its debt with private investors. Several protections are put in place for private investors via this plan, with the increased transparency from the country and the heightened scrutiny from the agencies meaning that countries can and will be returned to the normal rating system the moment they fail to comply with the measures put in place by the programme – meaning that investors will be notified as usual if the country cannot meet its financial obligations. With the support of all the parties concerned – investors, rating agencies, American and European legislators/regulators, and vulnerable countries – there is a theoretical chance that the credit rating impasse can be broken with the proposed programme.

The aim here is to highlight the relevant sections of the American and European legislative spheres that the proposed programme would affect. Legislators, rating agencies, and regulators would need to come together to implement the best legal tools at their disposal to make practicable changes that would provide the rating agencies with the legal flexibility to enact the programme (together with the right legal actions to guard against rating agency transgressive behaviour). The focus will be on the concept of methodological integrity, together with rating symbol consistency. The reason for this is that essentially, the claim from the rating agencies regarding downgrading vulnerable countries is that they are bound to, by law, because they need to say what they do and do what they say, that is, they have to state their methodologies in advance and stick to them. This is the crux of the matter for the purposes of this proposed programme because we are suggesting that the credit rating agencies should *change* their methodological and rating symbol approach, in a very temporary and purposeful way, for the benefit of vulnerable countries attached to multilateral programmes (and their creditors).

In the US, the task is much easier because sovereign ratings do not feature in the Dodd–Frank Act, and there is very little said about methodological integrity. We know from earlier in the chapter that this is because the EU has a very different relationship with the rating agencies because of its constitution and history. As such, in the Dodd–Frank Act, there are only a couple of sections to note. The first is the overriding structure of the legislative approach in relation to methodological integrity. Section 932 (r) states:

> 932 (r) – *The Commission shall prescribe rules, for the protection of investors and in the public interest, with respect to the procedures and methodologies, including qualitative and quantitative data and models, used by nationally recognized*

statistical rating organizations that require each nationally recognized statistical rating organization –

(1) to ensure that credit ratings are determined using procedures and methodologies, including qualitative and quantitative data and models, that are –

(A) *approved by the board of the nationally recognized statistical rating organization, a body performing a function similar to that of a board*; and
(B) *in accordance with the policies and procedures of the nationally recognized statistical rating organization for the development and modification of credit rating procedures and methodologies*;

(2) to ensure that when material changes to credit rating procedures and methodologies (including changes to qualitative and quantitative data and models) are made, that –

(A) *the changes are applied consistently to all credit ratings to which the changed procedures and methodologies apply*;
(B) to the extent that changes are made to credit rating surveillance procedures and methodologies, the changes are applied to then-current credit ratings by the nationally recognized statistical rating organization within a reasonable time period determined by the Commission, by rule; and
(C) *the nationally recognized statistical rating organization publicly discloses the reason for the change; and "(3) to notify users of credit ratings –*

(A) *of the version of a procedure or methodology, including the qualitative methodology or quantitative inputs, used with respect to a particular credit rating*;
(B) when a material change is made to a procedure or methodology, including to a qualitative model or quantitative inputs;
(C) when a significant error is identified in a procedure or methodology, including a qualitative or quantitative model, that may result in credit rating actions; and
(D) of the likelihood of a material change described in subparagraph (B) resulting in a change in current credit ratings.[21]

I have emphasised the relevant sections for us in the above. The emphasised excerpts show that the aim of the legislation is for the agencies to be transparent with their methodologies and to stick to them. Communicating the methodologies to the investing public is critical, and whilst changes are allowed, it is *vital* that these changes and the reasons for them are articulated clearly. This sentiment is continued in the next subsection of the section in the Act which focuses on the need for disclosures of forms that will accompany any credit rating to *explain* to the users of ratings the underlying reasons for the credit rating given, both for quantitative and qualitative content. In addition, credit rating agencies must declare any conflicts of interest that may have affected the ratings.

For a number of reasons, the above should be maintained. The need for transparency is key for vulnerable countries in order to allow the credit rating agencies to do their job as best they can and to provide the most accurate credit rating for investors. However, transparency is key *from* the credit rating agencies, and the changes made on behalf of this programme would need to be articulated fully, clearly, and arguably simply so that all investors can be informed about the programme and its aims, limitations, and processes. Therefore, those particular elements of the Dodd–Frank Act would not necessarily need to be changed, although allowing the agencies to implement the overlay would need to be recognised by lawmakers and regulators via the sections highlighted above, or they would need to be slightly amended should it be deemed too far outside the limits of those emphasised sections (it should be able to be applied though).

Another element of the programme is the inclusion of a different rating scale for the vulnerable countries on the programme to make clear to investors the changed nature of the ratings from the usual methodologies. We discussed that this was done in relation to the rating of structured finance products in the aftermath of the Financial Crisis, and it would need to be done here. An example could be that instead of the 'sf' moniker now attached to structured finance ratings to declare the delineation from usual ratings, the rating scale attached to the overlay could have 'CF' attached to it (for 'Common Framework'); another option could easily work just the same, of course. This is allowed under the Dodd–Frank Act because in Section 938 (a)(2), the Act says that the SEC shall require agencies to 'clearly define and disclose the meaning of any symbol used by the nationally recognised statistical rating organisation to denote a credit rating' and that (3) the agencies have to 'apply any symbol described in paragraph (2) in a manner that is consistent for all types of securities and money market instruments for which the symbol is used'. The Act continues by confirming that 'nothing in this section shall prohibit a nationally recognised statistical rating organisation from using distinct sets of symbols to denote credit ratings for different types of securities or money market instruments'. Thus, as long as a rating scale is used consistently, there is legal scope to develop a new rating scale and apply it to a particular set of securities. The problem comes in the form of differentiating between sovereign ratings of different sets of countries (i.e. those included in the multilateral initiatives and those not) which would need to be rectified by lawmakers.

In terms of direct legal sections in the Dodd–Frank Act, the premier legal instrument affecting the credit rating agencies, that is all that is applicable. As long as lawmakers allow the credit rating agencies to differentiate amongst a particular class of securities ratings, which they would need to do as above, then the other elements of the Act would remain applicable, in the sense of enforcing transparency and articulation of methodological changes. This would be important to maintain so that investors in vulnerable countries remain informed and protected via the programme.

In the EU, however, more would need to be done to accommodate the proposed programme.

In the first set of legislative regulations implemented in 2009, two Articles are of interest to us. In Article 10(3), the EU confirmed that

> When a credit rating agency issues credit ratings for structured finance instruments, it shall ensure that rating categories that are attributed to structured finance instruments are clearly differentiated using an additional symbol which distinguishes them from rating categories used for any other entities, financial instruments or financial obligations.[22]

This confirms, as the Dodd–Frank Act does, that the practice of developing rating monikers to be attached to ratings, with the aim of differentiating in the minds of investors, is a practice that is supported. However, in Article 8, the same issue that we encountered in the Dodd–Frank Act is revealed in the EU CRA I Regulation.

Article 8 focuses on the methodologies from the agencies and the transmission of them to the investing public. After mandating in Article 8(1) that methodologies, models, and key assumptions need to be made public, the Regulation goes on to say in subsection (2) that

> A credit rating agency shall adopt, implement, and enforce adequate measures to ensure that the credit ratings it issues are based on a thorough analysis of all the information that is available to it and that is relevant to its analysis according to its rating methodologies.

It says in subsection (3) that a credit rating agency shall use rating methodologies that are rigorous, systematic, continuous, and subject to validation based on historical experience, including back-testing. It concludes in subsection (6) by stating:

> When methodologies, models or key rating assumptions used in credit rating activities are changed, a credit rating agency shall:
>
> (a) immediately, using the same means of communication as used for the distribution of the affected credit ratings, disclose the likely scope of credit ratings to be affected;
> (b) review the affected credit ratings as soon as possible and no later than six months after the change, in the meantime placing those ratings under observation; and
> (c) re-rate all credit ratings that have been based on those methodologies, models or key rating assumptions if, following the review, the overall combined effect of the changes affects those credit ratings.

This is problematic for the implementation of the programme for two reasons. The first is that the ratings conducted by the agencies for the programme will be based on a new methodology of sorts; thus, the question arises as to whether there will be enough historic data available to back-test the new methods. Remember, the aim of the programme is for the agencies to rate the vulnerable countries in a *different* manner than they have before, complete with new levels of transparent data disclosure from the countries in question. The second problem comes in the form of subsection (6)(c), which calls for *all* credit ratings based upon a methodology that has been changed to be re-rated. The proposed programme's need for a new sovereign methodology could be interpreted as being a changed sovereign methodology that, according to the subsection, should then be applied to *all* sovereign credit ratings that have been given by the particular rating agency – this defeats the purpose of the programme. For these reasons, these particular sections would need to be considered by European legislators when amending the implementation of the programme.

In the 2011 amendment to the Regulation, the Articles identified above were not amended. The aim was, as we discussed earlier, to incorporate the newly formed ESMA into the credit rating Regulation. The one notable addition to the Regulation for us came in the amendment to Article 23, which stated unequivocally 'in carrying out their duties under this Regulation, ESMA, the Commission, or any public authorities of a Member State shall not interfere with the content of credit ratings or methodologies'.[23] This clarifies that it is the agencies who would need to develop the overlay as they see fit rather than have it dictated to them by legislation or regulation. In 2013, however, in response to the Sovereign Debt Crisis as discussed earlier in the chapter, the Articles identified above were amended.

The majority of amendments were to include reference to sovereign ratings in particular, and we know why. Yet, in relation to agencies altering their stated methodologies, in paragraph (2)(c), the Regulation says that an amendment was being inserted to say that 'a credit rating agency that intends to make a material change to, or use, new rating methodologies, models, or key rating assumptions which could have an impact on a credit rating shall publish the proposed material changes or proposed new rating methodologies on its website inviting stakeholders to submit comments for a period of one month together with a detailed explanation of the reasons for and the implications of the proposed material changes or proposed new rating methodologies'. It continues to confirm that the rating agency would need to inform ESMA of the proposed change immediately and publish the results of the public consultation. This is positive as it improves the transparency of the methodological process. For the programme, it would also be positive as it would invite public responses that could better define the methodology and force the agency in question to articulate how it would apply the methodology it had developed.

Furthermore, the Regulation prohibits the agencies from rating groups of countries and insists that any sovereign rating must be related to an individual country, with the reasoning being made clear and always needing to be related to information that has been disclosed by the rated entity (not without its consent) unless the information is widely and publicly available. The Regulation also enforces a calendar system for rating agencies to publish sovereign ratings, which needs to be done in advance, for a period of 12 months, with a maximum of three pre-described dates for unsolicited ratings (and they have to be on a Friday after the European markets close). Deviations from the schedule are prohibited except for specific reasons relating to other Articles in the Regulation. The aim of this approach is to stop contagion like that witnessed at the start of the Sovereign Debt Crisis. However, for the programme, it means that amendments would need to be made because the approach for the programme is based on a (potentially) increased number of ratings for the rated entities whilst within the programme to increase the protection for private creditors. The reason for the increased rate of rating updates, as mentioned earlier, is because the countries in the programme are of a high credit risk nature and are attempting to move away from the default zone of the rating scale – the cost for avoiding that and being able to renegotiate with private creditors via the programme is the increased scrutiny from the rating agencies.

Those are the sections of the EU CRA Regulations that would need to be considered. As you can see, they are similar to the Dodd–Frank Act's elements that would need to be considered, but perhaps more action would be needed by the European legislators solely based on the fact that they regulated the provision of sovereign ratings so closely but for obvious reasons.

5.4 Limitations

The preceding subsection outlined the areas of the existing legislative frameworks within the US and the EU that would need to be considered and/or altered for the programme to be legally implemented. The aim is to provide the rating agencies with the legal flexibility with which they can rate the countries attached to the multilateral debt treatment initiatives differently from other sovereigns. To do that, legislators would need to ensure two things. First, ensure that the flexibility is constrained and monitored adequately. Second, ensure that there are no other legal avenues for the rating agencies to be found liable for rating the sovereigns differently; protecting the rating agencies from liability for doing what the programme needs is *vital* because without that protection, they cannot fulfil their role in the imagined programme (as we are seeing in the current credit rating impasse). This will not be easy for legislators to 'swallow' given their experiences with the credit rating agencies in the past.

There is also the issue of scale. For the programme to be implemented, there are many moving parts which need to be moved at the same time. To provide legislative flexibility is one thing, but we would also need the support of private investors, sovereign debtors, and credit rating agencies. Inducting the credit rating agencies into this programme is probably the largest hurdle after the legislators because there is little direct and tangible upside for the agencies; their benefit lies in long-term positive regard for taking part in a programme that helps vulnerable sovereigns and the potential increase in the sovereign debt market that the programme can theoretically enable. However, can the rating agencies place their trust in the legal flexibility that is being asked from legislators? They would be under no obligation to provide credit ratings for the programme and cannot be compelled. To create an air of collaboration, it is important that the credit rating agencies have the chance to inform the legislative procedures required for the programme. It is also important that the building of the special methodologies and rating scales, as imagined by the programme, are heavily influenced by the credit rating agencies; the methodological underpinnings of that special approach cannot be forced upon credit rating agencies but need to be built in collaboration *with* them.

Finally, all of this needs to be done in good time. There is often a substantial lag from idea to implementation, and when positioned on a global scale and involving so many players, there is a high chance that the lag could be critically long. Vulnerable sovereigns need help now. However, the establishment of a programme like the one presented here allows for the capability to protect against future global shocks, and there *will be* future global shocks. The lack of a bankruptcy procedure at the global level means that vulnerable sovereign debtors are never far away from a crisis. Timing is everything. However, there also needs to be a reality check in terms of debt development. The reality is that the current way of working does not work. Lurching from debt crisis to debt crisis is not sustainable, and if the world (particularly the western world) is determined to include the developing world in the capital markets, then there needs to be the infrastructure to make that sustainable; at the moment, there is nothing close to achieving that aim. In the absence of an adequate international bankruptcy regime for sovereign debtors, this programme provides a system that allows sovereigns to renegotiate their debt obligations; at the very least, that revelation could reset the global order when it comes to the trajectory of the developing world.

5.5 Conclusion

The options for legislators, if they were to consider implementing the programme as devised by this book, are clear: make small amendments to existing legislation to guard against the effects of the programme for all participants (particularly rating agencies) or develop new legislation which could sit on top of the current legislative structure in both jurisdictions that could be applied in relation to multilateral initiatives.

The reasons for the development of the different legislative programmes in the US and the EU are clear and entirely rational. One decided to legislate against the causes of the Financial Crisis, and one went further to legislate against the effects of the Sovereign Debt Crisis in addition to the Financial Crisis. It all makes sense. However, this has resulted in a legislative rigidity that is now forcing credit rating agencies into a liability-related corner that it has no intention of fighting its way out of; it does not pay for the rating agencies to help the vulnerable countries, it can only cost them. To that end, this chapter aimed to indicate the areas of potential legislative reform that would be required to be reconsidered, or even slightly amended, to remove some of the rigidity. That removal of rigidity would technically allow the rating agencies to be more helpful in the overarching aim of breaking the credit rating impasse, as I have presented here in this book. However, the request for the reduction in legislative rigidity comes with a stark warning.

That warning is a very simple one: legislators must only reduce the rigidity of the legislation in a very specific and controlled manner. There is a reason the legislation was designed in such a rigid manner, and that is because of the constitution of the rating agencies' culture and environment. I am not a proponent of the argument that rating agencies and their people are fundamentally 'bad' – they are not. However, the role of the agencies, and the allure of transgressive behaviour that generates remarkable riches, can be hard for even the most moralistic amongst us to succumb to. The legislators need to know this. Vulnerable countries need the world's help in a systemic manner, and this book provides for a small intervention into that system. However, the world needs legislators to be prudent and vigilant – there cannot be a repeat of the mistakes of the mid-2000s in Europe. It is for legislators to find that balance, and they must do that if they are true to their word when they say they are invested in enabling the world's most vulnerable countries to return from the pandemic in the best shape possible.

Notes

1 Daniel Cash, *Regulation and the Credit Rating Agencies: Restraining Ancillary Services* (Routledge 2018).

2 For some of the seminal works on this particular subject, see: Patricia T. Langohr and Herwig M. Langohr, *The Rating Agencies and their Credit Ratings: What They Are, How They Work and Why They Are Relevant* (John Wiley & Sons 2008); Raquel G. Alcubilla and Javier Ruiz del Pozo, *Credit Rating Agencies on the Watch List: Analysis of European Regulation* (OUP 2012); Mohammed Hemraj, *Credit Rating Agencies: Self-Regulation, Statutory Regulation and Case Law Regulation in the United States and European Union* (Springer 2015); Andrea Miglionico, *The Governance of Credit Rating Agencies: Regulatory Regimes and Liability Issues* (Edward Elgar 2019).

3 Miglionico (n 2) 4.02.

4 Ibid 405.

5 Cash (n 1).

6 Miglionico (n 2) 4.08.

7 Ibid.

8 Hemraj (n 2) 100.

9 Greg Gordon, 'Industry Wrote Provision that Undercuts Credit-Rating Overhaul' (2013) *McClatchy* (Aug 7) https://web.archive.org/web/20130905063015/www.mcclatchydc.com/2013/08/07/198739/industry-wrote-provision-that.html#.Uidbt6ypeSo.

10 Miglionico (n 2) 4.25.

11 Danielle Carbone, 'The Impact of the Dodd-Frank Act's Credit Rating Agency Reform on Public Companies' (2010) *Insights: The Corporate & Securities Law Advisor* (Sept).

12 Steven G. Brody and Cynthia A. Hanawalt, 'Dodd-Frank Act's Impact on Rating Agencies as the ABS Market Continues to Evolve' (2010) *Martindale* (Dec 16) www.martindale.com/legal-news/article_bingham-mccutchen-llp_1206318.htm.

13 Alcubilla and del Pozo (n 2) 47.

14 Miglionico (n 2) 5.04.
15 Ibid.
16 Mads Andenas and Iris H-Y. Chiu, *The Foundations and Future of Financial Regulation: Governance for Responsibility* (Routledge 2013) 231.
17 Philip R. Lane, 'The European Sovereign Debt Crisis' (2012) 26 *Journal of Economic Perspectives* 3 49–68, 49.
18 Norbert Gaillard, 'Credit Rating Agencies and the Eurozone Crisis: What Is the Value of Sovereign Ratings?' (2013) *Voxeu* (Sept 9) https://voxeu.org/article/credit-rating-agencies-and-eurozone-crisis-what-value-sovereign-ratings.
19 Phoebus L. Athanassiou and Angelos T. Vouldis, *The European Sovereign Debt Crisis: Breaking the Vicious Circle between Sovereigns and Banks* (Routledge 2021); Caroline de la Porte and Elke Heins (eds), *The Sovereign Debt Crisis, the EU and Welfare State Reform* (Palgrave Macmillan 2016); Christian Scheiger and Jose M Magone (eds), *The Effects of the Eurozone Sovereign Debt Crisis* (Routledge 2015).
20 Miglionico (n 2) 4.27
21 *The Dodd-Frank Wall Street Reform and Consumer Protection Act* (2010) H.R. 4173 (emphasis added).
22 Regulation (EC) No 1060/2009.
23 Regulation (EC) No 513/2011.

6 The Future for Africa

6.1 Introduction

The title of this brief and final chapter is exceptionally arrogant. It is arrogant because there is no telling the future of the African continent, as well as the fact that different countries on the continent face very different futures. The title has been selected only for bringing the work together from where we started earlier in the book. The first chapter analysed the history of major debt treatment initiatives on the continent, and we could not do that without first looking at the concept of colonialism and its devastating impact. Across several eras and for very different reasons, Africa has been the centre of the world. Leaving aside the obvious anthropological significance of the continent, the political and economic significance of the continent has been substantial over several different time periods. During colonial times on the continent, it sat in the middle of major political, economic, and militaristic tussles between global superpowers. Today, the continent is in precisely the same position, albeit with different actors.

In this chapter, we will see a new colonialism, in a way, being played out on the African continent. We will look at, in turn, the tussling between the Chinese, American, and European governments with a precise focus on the French. At the heart of the scramble is the global need for precious natural resources that the African continent contains, although the new dimension of the global battle for influence between China and America has developed new and impactful strategies that are affecting the continent. In addition, we shall see how newly developed 'global initiatives' may affect the African continent, all seemingly aimed at 'developing' the continent that is home to some of the world's most valuable resources. In this sense, we shall see how the political domain, that is, the internal mechanics of the democratic societies versus the autocratic societies, affect the capability to provide development support to the world's developing economies.

One of the most important reasons for this chapter's inclusion is that it is an important backdrop for our analysis. The aim throughout the book has been to alter the lens with which we view the current plight of some of the world's most vulnerable countries and the attempts to alleviate the pressure. What we

DOI: 10.4324/9781003261223-7

will see is that there is a larger 'game' being played, for want of a better word, that affects everything related to the continent. For example, it is alleged later in the chapter via the excellent work of Professor Horace Campbell that the rise of the private creditor and the move towards the capital markets was no fluke, with the multilateral institutions being identified as having particular mandates to promote private capital across the developing world. In contrast, arguments have been put forward that suggest the constant focus on the negative effects of Chinese investment on the continent are predominantly smear campaigns to aid with the western, principally American, quest for dominance in the region. There are counterarguments to these positions as well, of course, which further add complexity to understanding what the continent is facing. We will examine these issues, but the underlying sentiment of a continent that continues to be caught in the crosshairs of the financial and political elite is vital to remember as we continue.

6.2 Democracy and Autocracy in the African Continent

How a country is governed has an impact on its relationship with the rest of the world. There is no one right way to govern a country, of course, but the dominant dichotomy on the continent is between democratically run countries and those governed in an autocratic manner. Researchers and onlookers have been keen to monitor the development of the two styles across the African continent for some time, and for good reason. The majority of western-based research seeks to examine the rates of improvement or decline in governments considered to be truly democratic in nature. Several 'indicators' have been identified that, when ranked, intend to show how strong a country's democracy is. Regrettably, it is often the case that research into this is based on the understanding that democracy is 'good' and autocracy is 'bad', which is based on the researcher's position more than anything else, but we shall not delve too deeply into that here; the point being that impartiality is often missing from research endeavours. What is important, however, is how that research feed into much larger narratives.

In terms of the African experience, Kpundeh states that the early interventions from the multilateral institutions in the early 1990s were not only to do with enacting financial 'structural adjustments' but also political adjustments. The constitution of the multilateral institutions such as the IMF and the World Bank makes it clear as to what political approach was favoured, but the strategy was to attach political reform to the financial assistance. That conditionality is almost a standard across all of the western financial aid programmes but differs in form:

> The condition that political reforms be undertaken is now attached at least rhetorically to almost all western aid. Actual donor practices vary: France proposes greater liberty and democracy, Great Britain recommends good government, the United States focuses on good governance, Japan talks

> about linking aid to reductions in military expenditures. Yet, regardless of the approach, there is increasingly strong agreement among donors that political reforms in Africa must result in reduced corruption and more financial accountability, better observance of human rights, independent media and an independent judiciary, participatory politics, and a liberalised market economy in order to move closer to the ultimate goal of meaningful economic growth and economy.[1]

Whilst the aforementioned factors are not the only way in which one can experience economic and market growth, the conditionality is clear. However, the question becomes whether that conditionality can lead to the spreading of the chosen political form from western donors.

The reality, unfortunately, is that democracy's strength is only as strong as what the system can provide for the country. In times of growth, countries that do not have a historic connection to one political approach over another tend to do well in terms of developing democratic systems. However, when financial fortunes are reversed, we witness sharp declines in the strength of those democratic indicators mentioned earlier. For instance, before the pandemic, it was noted that more than half of all Africans on the continent lived in 'functioning multiparty electoral democracies that are demonstrably freer than were the military or one-party regimes that previously dominated the continent'. Although the strength of democratic indicators had lessened since the peak in 2006,[2] the pre-pandemic situation for democracy on the continent was relatively positive.

However, the Financial Crisis affected almost every nation in one way or another. Researchers noted a general global decline in the strength of democratic indicators, with even established democracies undergoing periods of unprecedented stress since the peak of the Financial Crisis.[3] It is not surprising given the historic amount of wealth extraction[4] that took place during that era, which left many within democratic societies to pay for the misdeeds of the financial elite. The African continent, with its unstable political foundations, was to be no exception.

The narrative discussed above is perhaps vindicated when we look at the experience of African societies just before and during the pandemic. Though there are 'bright spots' across the continent, 'like the rise of more resilient opposition movements in the Democratic Republic of Congo and Uganda', Cheeseman wrote in 2019, 'elsewhere on the continent, as in Tanzania and Zambia, repression is on the rise'.[5] It is interesting to note that research undertaken in 2019, a year before the onset of the pandemic, reveals that whilst there was not a 'collapse' of democracy on the continent, there were certainly 'difficulties'. Cheeseman cites the Bertelsmann Transformation Index, which measures the strength of particular democratic indicators, and shows that between 2015 and 2017, 'the average score for every measure of political change in Africa fell . . . this means there was an overall decline in the quality of political participation, rule of law and the capacity of the state in a number of areas'.[6]

As we shall see next, one significant element of the pandemic was the ability of autocratic states to impose restrictions and amendments to constitutions in the name of COVID-19 prevention, but this was already taking place before the onset of the pandemic. Again, Cheeseman notes that:

> The stability of democratic institutions, as well as political and social integration, also declined. Some of these changes are relatively small. But they are also consistent with a decade of democratic backsliding and the entrenchment of authoritarianism. In line with these trends, more countries moved towards authoritarian rule than democracy during this period. Most notably, growing government abuses in Uganda and Mozambique led both to be downgraded to 'moderate autocracies'. Similar developments in Burundi and Zimbabwe saw them falling to the index's least democratic classification: 'hard-line autocracies'. Nothing better epitomises the curtailing of democratic checks and balances than the removal of presidential term limits, and age limits for the head of state in some countries. For now, restrictions have been respected in more countries than they have been abandoned. But 2015 to 2017 saw the continuation of a worrying trend as leaders in the continent's most authoritarian states used their control of political systems to set themselves up as presidents for life. Following Djibouti (2011), the Republic of Congo (2015), and Burundi (2015), term limits on President Paul Kagame were circumvented in Rwanda in 2017. In Uganda President Yoweri Museveni – who freed himself from term limits in 2006 – successfully manoeuvred the passage of legislation that led to the removal of age limits in late 2017.[7]

Mbaku explains that this process of changing the constitution to maintain power is called a 'constitutional coup' and indicates that several African countries have recently experienced this, including Togo, Uganda, Chad, Cameroon, Rwanda, Burundi, and Egypt.[8] Constitutional coups are easier to pull off in a pandemic, but there are many other ways in which authoritarian leaders are expanding their power and influence. Munshi describes how 'democratic backsliding' is increasing on the continent under the cover of the pandemic, with authorities in Niger shutting down the internet and charging political officials with attempting to overthrow the government, security forces in Chad killing opposition leaders, and changes in electoral law in Benin essentially banning opposition leaders from challenging. Furthermore, and in relation to the later sector of the chapter, he notes that Francophone countries are suffering the worst from this backsliding, with France overlooking such regressive developments because 'France is more vested in the presidents [and] presidential candidates who will uphold France's interest'.[9]

Other examples include the blocking of particular social media sites in Senegal,[10] which is a serious problem on the continent. For example, Cheeseman revealed in 2020 that in Tanzania, western companies had been actively assisting in political repression across the country to keep the incumbent president in power, with even more sophisticated than the usual internet bans that are witnessed elsewhere:

> Mobile phone companies had caved to a government demand to filter and block messages containing certain terms associated with the country's main opposition party. One of those companies was Vodacom Tanzania, part of the Vodafone Group, a multinational company headquartered in Britain. Despite proudly proclaiming their commitment to promoting 'inclusion for all', 'operating responsibly' and contributing to the 'UN SDGs' on their website, a western company aided an authoritarian leader to undermine freedom of speech.[11]

Cheeseman suggests that this is just one example, with western technological companies playing active parts in maintaining repression in Bahrain, Qatar, Oman, Saudi Arabia, Kuwait, Yemen, Sudan, and Tunisia amongst many others with regards to issues such as secular discourse, sex and GLBT, and anonymity.

With democracy in retreat, there has been intense focus on who to blame. The failure of the West's model via the Financial Crisis has largely escaped the blame for whatever reason, though it has been suggested that 'Donald Trump has made dictatorship hip again'.[12] That aside, there is one entity that has received much of the blame for the difficulties democracy is facing on the continent, and an extraordinary amount of research has gone into explaining why that is the case. That entity is China.

6.3 The Global Battle for Influence in the African Continent

China forms part of a three-pronged analysis here. China has a very complicated relationship with the African continent that has often been oversimplified to develop a negative narrative about their role and intention. However, the complicated elements of the relationship are being revealed by astute researchers seeking to develop a more holistic narrative.

China's role on the continent began to significantly expand in the wake of the Financial Crisis. The early 2010s represented a sea-change in the direction of Chinese influence on the continent, with Iwilade confirming in 2014 that 'China is Africa's largest new investor, and the value of its two-way trade – at almost $200 billion in 2012 – is second only to that of the United States'.[13] Since then, that investment has grown significantly – one estimate puts this at just over $150 billion from 2000 to 2019.[14] Predictably, that rate of investment has upset the status quo on the continent and led to warnings about the potential negative effects that could come from it.

Early concerns centred around the agenda of the Chinese state and its willingness to overlook issues. For example, Iwilade, citing Joseph, shows us that the concerns spanned different issues: '"China's growing presence has been complicating prospects for further democratisation in Africa" because it often ignores governance and human rights problems and makes investments to strengthen autocratic regimes'.[15] This concern is coupled with the concern that China is and was participating in a 'scramble' for precious resources. These viewpoints are evidenced by the instances where China has invested, predominantly, in resource-rich countries like Angola and has participated in selling arms to countries that commit human rights abuses on a large scale, like in Sudan. Iwilade calls for holistic understandings to be undertaken, and this is the right approach. For example, whilst China has sold small arms to countries like Sudan that have gone on to be used in human rights abuses in the country, China is the second-largest arms seller to the continent, behind the US.[16]

China's impact on the continent cannot be generalised. Whilst in some countries, the support for autocratic governments is clear – and this is usually when the autocratic government rules a resource-rich country – there are also instances where China provides for peacekeeping efforts in countries in conflict or for the increase in democracy in countries that have chosen that path. China has a foreign policy of political non-conditionality or non-interference, and its range of approaches almost confirms that. For this reason, China has been identified by some as being a 'net-promoter' of democracy on the African continent.[17] This understanding fully challenges the dominant narrative. Although China's investment on the continent slowed during the pandemic, it still has a strong relationship with it. For example, China recently announced its '2035 Vision for China–African Cooperation', which partners its own programme for becoming a global leader and influencer by 2035, in time for the Communist Party's century in power celebrations. The cooperation envisioned takes the form of partnerships in development agenda, trade/investment/financing, industrial cooperation, green cooperation, health, people-to-people exchanges, peace and security, and corporation on global governance.[18] Earlier, in Chapter 3, we learned how the Chinese President sees this partnership as something much deeper than an economic trading partnership when he stated that 'no one could hold back the Chinese people or the African people as we march towards rejuvenation', which suggests a much deeper connection than anything superficial; China's narrative of bringing traditionally western-oppressed peoples together is key to their strategy. However, the real issue here is whether that understanding of the global order holds up under scrutiny.

Many will argue one way or the other, and that is their right. However, several facts paint a revealing picture. Today, there are two global superpowers: the US and China. In Africa, given China's growing connection with the continent, the US has started to build its influence on the region even more to counter the Chinese position. For example, Schewe concisely describes how

> it has escaped nobody's notice that the longest-term strategic threat to the United States in Africa is not terrorism. China's influence is spreading without military occupation [or] elaborate social research . . . rather, China will let its economic power speak for itself.

Furthermore, 'unlike US and European investors focused on the short-term, [Chinese] state-owned enterprises make the majority of such investments, with the "objective of forming long-lasting relationships with the communities and governments with which they cooperate"'.[19] Whilst Schewe makes clear that the endeavours of the Chinese are not charitable in nature, he points out that China has changed the foreign policy landscape on the continent to a point where the US cannot compete and its age-old approach of militaristic dominance is starting to show signs of wear. Whilst the Chinese investment in infrastructure projects is not universally welcomed in Africa (often they are white elephants and have been built to be built [or for political gain], rather than for need),[20] it is also the case that 'the US military is using piecemeal programs to cover over a frustrating cycle of counterterrorism raids and surveillance that will never gain the public legitimacy necessary to produce results'.[21]

As the Chinese take a high-level diplomatic approach to the continent, with Xi Jinping featuring heavily in the relationship between the two, the American approach is much different. US military operations are underway on the continent in more than 20 countries, and the US has nearly 30 military bases on the continent, despite claiming that it has a 'light footprint' on the continent.[22] Its military presence is conducted through 'AFRICOM', which stands for US Africa Command. Born in 2007, it is headquartered in Stuttgart rather than on the continent. Perhaps in revealing the US relationship with the continent, its leaders are considered the face of the US presence and visit the continent significantly more than US Presidents or senior politicians have.[23] In addition to AFRICOM, the US military presence extends to its intelligence services, with the CIA also having a considerable presence on the continent.[24] The other interesting element, however, is that AFRICOM has a limited amount of personnel but a footprint much larger than its staffing levels would suggest. They achieve this by contracting private military operations which alter the way in which it impacts the continent. For example, as a heavy militaristic presence is no longer needed on the continent, it instead embarks upon a 'financialisation and information warfare' approach, which is made up of 'cyber warriors and private military companies'. Campbell argues that AFRICOM was set up only to counter Chinese interest in the region and that destabilisation via a variety of methods is one of the key aims of the command.[25]

Campbell, a specialist in this field of research, is absolutely scathing regarding the purpose of the US presence in the region. He begins by saying that 'the US notion of security in Africa is influenced by the interests of the financial oligarchs and corporate moguls, supported by the foreign policy establishment'. However, he builds a picture of a concerted approach to assert dominance by extraction and destabilisation which, if the research on the reality of the Chinese approach is to be believed, is in direct opposition to the Chinese approach:

> The IMF and the World Bank had pushed Africa hard towards privatization and development of capital markets, yet the continent was not completely enmeshed in the formal international capital markets. Illicit production

> of minerals, illicit trade in resources and the laundering of illicit gains had become a central feature of the way Africa was integrated into the international system. US policy makers had noted the dominance of European capitalists in resource extraction from Africa in the 1990s. The Clinton Administration embarked on the Africa Crisis Response Initiative (ACRI) and the Africa Growth and Opportunity Act (AGOA) as two public initiatives to facilitate America's domination of Africa's political economy.[26]

Campbell is keen to remind us of hypocrisy in what the world is told and what really happens. For instance, despite all the claims of pushing for democracy on the continent and countering forces that do not respect human rights etc., the reality is that the US government has its fingerprints on a number of international crimes, ranging from footprints in Guinea to aid US oil majors, covering up the murder of Patrice Lumumba, the propping-up of Mobutu Sese Seko, overthrowing Kwama Nkrumah, destabilising South Africa in favour of Apartheid, and the instance of the Rwandan genocide in relation to which the US government created the ACRI to support humanitarianism whilst simultaneously campaigning to the UN to withdraw troops from Rwanda *in the middle* of the genocide as more than one million people perished.[27] It is no wonder that Nelson Mandela's disregard for the ACRI was absolute.

Campbell explains other examples of this approach, such as the remarkable account of the destruction of Libya, infinitely much better than I could, and I implore you to read his work if you are interested.[28] It is clear that the US military is the spearhead of the American relationship with the continent, and whilst countering China is a relatively recent goal, its ultimate mission is to 'open markets for the US private sector'.[29] However, Campbell suggests that the real point of contention between the two superpowers is that China 'has alternative cooperation arrangements outside the dollar'. Anti-Chinese literature argues that China is offering African governments non-conditional loans that circumvent the American objective of tying governmental reform to the financial aid and investment that many countries require. However, the alternative viewpoint, as we have heard from the Chinese President, is that China and Africa's relationship is cooperative, not transactional.

Nevertheless, there are two competing approaches on display here: financial and militaristic. In the French approach, we see a third way. Whilst it is tempting to suggest the 'third way' is a European way, this would not be accurate; it would fit into the analysis of influence coming from different regions and cultures, but the reality is that although certain European economies such as the German and Dutch have interests in the continent, none has a relationship with the continent quite like the French.

The Fifth French Republic, established in 1958 by Charles de Gaulle, has a long history with the African continent that predates its 'birth'. Its colonial relationship was documented earlier in the book, but since colonialism officially ended in the 1960s and 1970s, differing approaches have been taken by the French. Nevertheless, as Medushevskiy and Shishkina suggest, 'at all stages, the use of camouflaged mechanisms of paternalism by France remained unchanged, despite the leaders' constant statements about the termination of neo-colonial practices'.[30] This understanding is useful because it becomes a useful lens with which to assess the French relationship with the continent.

The core concept when assessing the relationship between the two is the concept of 'Françafrique', a term generated by the first president of Côte d'Ivoire, F. Houfouet-Boigny, to explain the phenomenon of former French colonies seeking to maintain a positive relationship with the French. It is often used to refer to a group of countries that are said to be within the French sphere of influence on the continent, including Senegal, Côte d'Ivoire, Burkina Faso, Togo, Benin, Niger, Mali, Republic of the Congo, Gabon, Chad, Central African Republic, Cameroon, Madagascar, Comoros, Djibouti, the Democratic Republic of Congo, Burundi, and Rwanda. Françafrique became a project for the French, and de Gaulle put in place plans to elevate the project and the relationship with the former colonies. As part of the project, the colonies would retain a privileged position with the French, but in return, the French would have exclusive access to African resources and marketplaces. This project was then expanded to include the former colonies of the Belgians, the Spanish, and later the British. Unsurprisingly, judging by the terms set out above, numerous researchers have shown that this process was littered with corruption.[31]

Officially, the model of Françafrique no longer exists, with President Hollande declaring the end of the project in 2012. However, since then, France has conducted several military operations in the 'former' sphere of influence, and its companies still retain access to the most precious of commodities in the sphere. It has a strong recent record of propping-up dictators who are supportive of the French within the sphere[32] and has openly and consciously turned a blind eye to atrocities across the sphere, especially in Congo; unsurprisingly again, the French oil major Total is the largest oil producer in Congo. In addition, a large number of countries in the French sphere are deemed by international onlookers to be 'not free' in terms of their political makeup, further highlighting contradictions in stated approaches from the French.

Melly and Darracq explain how the French are not just innocent bystanders as the French 'wield a level of influence that it cannot command anywhere else in the world. In crisis situations, Paris is still seen as a key source of diplomatic, military, and financial pressure on or support for the countries in the region'.[33] The scholars suggest there are three major reasons for the French to continue their interest in the region:

- [The Francosphere] accounts for 3% of France's exports and remains an important supplier of oil and metals – uranium from Niger is particularly strategic for energy security as about one-quarter of France's electricity production depends on it. French companies are particularly strong in sectors such as logistics, port and rail operations, telecoms, shipping, banking and air transport; they also have significant interests in tropical commodities and agriculture.

- At least 240,000 French nationals are registered as residing in Africa.
- French engagements with African states have played an important role in sustaining its image as a major power. African countries can be a valuable source of supportive votes at the UN, and they have been key allies for France and fellow EU members in international negotiations on certain global issues, notably climate change.[34]

Despite arguments in the press that the concept of the French having a controlling interest in the sphere of countries identified is wholly inaccurate (arguments which are in a small group),[35] the sphere is growing with the French courting the cooperation of countries such as Nigeria, Kenya, and Ethiopia.[36] Furthermore, the French have come in for extraordinary criticism for their continuation of what appear to be underhanded practices to maintain economically extractive practices. The US State Department has said that the French policies in the region are 'one of the serious obstacles to the development of African democracy' (citing the French support for Charles Taylor in Liberia and Juvenal Habyariman whose regime organised the Rwandan genocide), whilst the Italian Vice-Prime Minister Luigi Di Maio accused France of continuing to colonise Africa and even called on the EU to impose sanctions on the French (which, of course, it did not). Other Italian senior politicians called for action, with one saying that France is 'only engaged in pumping out the natural resources in Africa'.[37]

The intra-competition within Europe reveals a fractured pan-European offering, which puts the many seemingly positive EU-based endeavours into a very different light. Irrespective of this, the French approach is a major factor on the continent. With this approach operating at the same time as the American and Chinese approaches, it is almost impossible to forecast the future for the African continent. What is useful, however, is to use these approaches as lenses with which to understand the continent better.

6.4 Global Initiatives Competing With Each Other

We have already reviewed the concept of the belt-and-road initiative and understand that it is a central component of China's foreign policy. Its success, however, and it has been successful across several recognised indicators, has caused issues. China is in the process of doing something the West has never done: impose its influence without subjugation and loss of life on a large scale. There are perhaps two reasons for this. First, as China would propose, the BRI represents a true partnership that seeks to provide assistance for development without the imposition of political and cultural interference; there are no 'structural adjustments' for the Chinese. We already know that China views the development of the world's emerging economies as a rebalancing of financial, political, and cultural imbalances that the West has been ever so keen to foster and exploit. However, there may be a more technical reason for China's success.

What we are seeing being played out on the global stage is, essentially, an ideological reality: autocratic regimes can do things that democratic regimes cannot, and vice-versa. The belt-and-road initiative *is* Xi Jinping's initiative, and he is utilising the order of his society to deliver it. For example, in a democratic society, there are limits to how much a government can provide for the development of other nations, and it cannot compel private entities to provide support for such endeavours. In China, Xi Jinping does not have this problem. Whilst China has remarkable reserves that it needs to deploy and wants to do so away from US Treasuries, the reality is that his authority since his inauguration has been consolidated beyond what was thought possible, not lessened. In the US, as just one example, the political landscape has lurched from the left, to the right, and to the left again during Xi's time in office, which means having a coordinated and agreed-upon foreign policy of development is simply not possible. In the EU, the very nature of the Union means that developing a concerted approach to external development is similarly unlikely. We can see this ideological reality in two particular examples.

The EU and the G7 have decided that the BRI can no longer rule supreme in the development arena. In 2021, the European Commission (EC) launched the 'Global Gateway', which was revealed by the EC as a new strategy

> to boost smart, clean and secure links in digital, energy and transport and strengthen health, education and research systems across the world. It stands for sustainable and trusted connections that work for people and the planet, to tackle the most pressing global challenges, from climate change and protecting the environment, to improving health security and boosting competitiveness and global supply chains.[38]

This launch coincided with the bloc's Indo-Pacific Strategy which presented the reality that the EU was seeking to bolster its influence outside of its own borders; this was seen as a serious 'pivot' from its usual approach because the EU has 'historically struggled to carry a substantive weight outside of the bloc's neighbourhood'.[39] To do this, the EU has said that it is mobilising up to €300 billion in investment between 2021 and 2027.

In her opening address regarding the launching of the Global Gateway, President of the EC, Ursula von der Leyen said:

> COVID-19 has shown how interconnected the world we live in is. As part of our global recovery, we want to redesign how we connect the world to build forward better. The European model is about investing in both hard and soft infrastructure, in sustainable investments in digital, climate and energy, transport, health, education and research, as well as in an enabling environment guaranteeing a level playing field. We will support smart investments in quality infrastructure, respecting the highest

> social and environmental standards, in line with the EU's democratic values and international norms and standards. The Global Gateway Strategy is a template for how Europe can build more resilient connections with the world.[40]

The initiative is built upon six key principles. As well as being aligned to major global initiatives such as the Paris Agreement and the UN's Agenda 2030 and its Sustainable Development Goals, the six principles are designed to be central pillars to the development, implementation, and legacy of the Global Gateway:

1 Democratic values and high standards
2 Good governance and transparency
3 Equal partnerships
4 Green and clean
5 Security focused
6 Catalysing private sector investment[41]

There are several takeaways from these principles. First, there is a clear conditionality to the Global Gateway, and ultimately, the Global Gateway needs to be seen as the EU promoting its interests in a changing world.[42] This is not surprising, but the conditionality that is attached to the initiative is representative of the key differences between the Global Gateway and, say, the BRI. It is clear that the EU sees itself as the defender of democracy on the global stage[43] (despite containing members that are clearly not aligned to that principle, e.g. Hungary), and the Global Gateway is, therefore, clearly a vehicle to spread that influence on the global stage. Second is also clearly a vehicle for attempting to expand the influence of the private sector around the world and particularly in developing economies. Yet, it is its perceived challenge to the BRI that has raised the most eyebrows because whilst it is understandable to want to challenge the Chinese in the development arena, the question then becomes can the EU achieve that aim?

Von der Leyen did not hold back when explaining the Global Gateway's opposition to the BRI. Despite the following not being included in the press release from the European Commission, the reality is that the anti-Chinese sentiment cannot be contained within the EU, and commentators and onlookers were immediately onto the scent. She said:

> We are good at financing roads. But it does not make sense for Europe to build a perfect road between a Chinese-owned copper mine and a Chinese-owned harbour.[44]

Of course, this is rational, despite the fact that it shows that the Europeans are not necessarily considering the effect that the initiative may have on the recipients as their primary concern. As we shall see in the remainder of this chapter, the Global Gateway is not the only new developmental initiative being proposed at the moment; the G7, led by the US, has launched the clunkily titled 'Build Back Better World' initiative that is being shortened to B3W. We will analyse this next, but the sentiment is the same – a 'counter offensive to the BRI'.[45]

If we use Africa as a case in point, then it is clear that the level of competition for influence on the global scene has been seriously ratcheted up in the last couple of decades. The failure of the Western version of capitalism in the 2000s sent signals to the global infrastructure, and that message was acted upon. China took its chance to consolidate its place as a global superpower by imposing an ideology that, whilst based clearly in self-interest, seeks to provide assistance without ideological conditionality. This action led to a reaction, and the recent announcements by the EU and the G7 represent that reaction. However, critics have argued that this competition is 'somewhat overblown'. Medinilla et al., in presenting this argument that is against the grain in terms of the narratives that are being pushed by the majority, suggest that the European and Chinese utilise very different business models when approaching the concept of development on the African continent. They argue that the EU and EU Member States have a developmental objective and use public funding to crowd in private finance to focus on competitive and decentralised solutions, whereas the Chinese focus on pumping massive investment into large-scale infrastructure projects. The clearly Euro-centric understanding is that the Europeans' footprint is less visible than the Chinese footprint but just as valuable.[46] This may be the case and, if it is, it is likely down to the differing histories of the two entities, as well as their differing connections with the regions they are both trying to 'develop'. However, the relatively lesser experience of the Chinese in terms of foreign development is reducing all the time, and as a result, the BRI is evolving day by day.

This is causing a particular effect. The convergence of the two approaches, as presented by Medinilla et al. above, is said to be unavoidable because the Chinese have already substantially reduced the level of their investment into BRI-recipient countries, with the aim being to invest in a wiser and more targeted manner than just large-scale infrastructure projects whilst also taking a 'greener' approach to its investments. The researchers suggest that this will bring the BRI closer to the stated aims of the European and American proposed approaches, but this has the potential to lead to conflict.

Sticking with Africa, it is abundantly clear that the demand for such an approach is exceptionally high, even before we take the recovery from the pandemic into account. When we consider the issue of renewable energy, Africa has the capacity to lead the way in the development of the sector, with the right support. To that end, both China and the West are positioning themselves to be the partner of choice, although it has been argued that what the continent needs is not one or the other, but both. It has been suggested that there is space for collaboration, with the technical developments and bureaucratic flexibility of the Chinese being able to complement the experience of delivering highly competent blended finance offerings by the Europeans.[47] However, this will not be as easy as the scholars predict because what underlies the relationship between the two is a distinct ideological difference that cannot be underplayed. In this sense, the viewpoints of the two actors are telling. The Chinese have made it clear that it would be open to working with the Europeans and Americans with their initiatives, whilst also suggesting there is plenty of space for the two to assist with the BRI in bringing a larger scale of development to the developing world.[48] We can choose whether we believe the Chinese in their sentiment, but their narrative is wildly different to their Western counterparts, with the Chinese Foreign Minister imploring the US, but by proxy, the Europeans as well, to focus on the developing world to build a 'family of openness, inclusiveness, innovation, growth, connectivity, and win-win cooperation' rather than turn said regions into ones of conflict and confrontation.[49] However, the EU has taken a different stance with its clear agenda to discredit the BRI and present itself as a higher standard of assistance. The Chinese have been clear in their response to the EU, with the Chinese arguing that the EU's main goal with the Global Gateway is not to improve developing nations but to challenge the Chinese.[50]

If we accept this argument, then there is plenty of evidence to support it. The narrative of the EU has been blunt to say the least, and it is has been said that the reason for the EU developing the initiative primarily to challenge the BRI is a simple one: the Global Gateway reflects 'changing EU foreign interests, but can also be seen as an expression of a deep-rooted sense of loss of control in the relations with developing countries it has always considered as part of the EU's direct sphere of influence'.[51] This needs to be compared to the reality that despite what the Europeans may think, the BRI is beneficial to the countries that have participated and is in very high demand. This also needs to be aligned with the reality that despite the scaremongering from European and American 'hawks' on the growing influence of China, China is not the leading developer in many of the regions cited by those onlookers – Japan has a much larger developmental footprint.[52] It is not difficult to see why critics are suggesting that the EU is more concerned with being seen to counter China as 'standing up' for democracy rather than genuinely benefiting the nations and peoples it claims to want to aid. Furthermore, the EU has arguably fallen for a nuanced trap set for it, whether consciously or unconsciously, by the Chinese. Research suggests that the BRI, with its lack of conditionality and ideological browbeating, has been met with a sigh of relief from the developing world and is at the core of the BRI's impressive and growing demand.[53] The EU, with its constant referral to 'standards' and the correct way of doing things, is arguably building a case *against* itself in the eyes of the developing. The sentiment of being anti-Chinese may garner support at home but is not being received well around the world.[54]

We have looked at the issues with the Global Gateway from an ideological stance, but the reality is that the technical details of the Global Gateway are perhaps even more damaging to its success. For example, every commentator has noted that so far, *very little* detail has been provided. Of the detail that has been provided, the fact that the €300 billion to be spent by the Global Gateway is not new funding, but already committed funds simply being repackaged, is not promising. This is one of two reasons that Gavas and Pleck label the Global Gateway as a 'paper tiger'. The second is the reality that a large amount of the success of the initiative depends on leveraging private capital, and that capital is more than aware of the risks in investing in infrastructure projects around the world in places that have increased financial risk since the pandemic and who were deemed financially risky anyway. The lack of detail on how the initiative will seek to encourage that private capital into the equation has caused critics to further predict a lack of success.

Other initiatives that seemingly were developed to counter the BRI have not succeeded.[55] For instance, South Korea, Japan, India, and Taiwan have major connectivity initiatives in place,[56] and in the US, in 2019, President Trump alongside his counterparts from Japan and Australia developed the 'Blue Dot Network', also aimed at fostering a digital revolution in many different parts of the world.[57] However, these initiatives seek to establish their own way in areas where the BRI has not been strong so far. This will likely change as the BRI evolves to focus on digital, medical, and green revolutions, but the point is that a concerted effort that truly embraces the breadth of the agenda the Chinese have set for themselves has yet to be developed by anybody else, and it is likely for good reason. One reason may be that it is not possible to achieve what is required when in a democratic system because there is too much change and upheaval to projects that is witnessed when the electorate can and does change the political direction of the state. However, it could also be something much deeper, in that the *sentiment* is too different. We must reserve judgement on the sentiment of the Chinese with the BRI because we must do that with all offerings. We also must reserve judgement because the BRI clearly puts the Chinese at an advantage over those it connects with. However, *how* that advantage is developed and enjoyed is the key issue. The political impartiality that has been demonstrated by the Chinese is in direct opposition to the ideological conditionality consistently proposed by the West, and the rest of the world is seemingly signalling its acceptance or rejection of that approach in how it moves towards the BRI or other initiatives; the BRI's popularity is not just because it provides for developmental assistance but because it has, at least as a veneer if nothing else, a semblance of cooperation which is simply lacking from the West's offerings; the Global Gateway seems to be no different. However, this has not stopped the G7 from developing their own response to the BRI, almost to be expected, and their offering is even less detailed than the Global Gateway but still potentially impactful for the African continent.

In 2021, the G7 announced, whilst at their meeting in Corbis Bay, UK, that they were 'determined to beat COVID-19 and build back better'.[58] This determination was guided by 'our enduring ideals as free open societies and democracies and by our commitment to multilateralism'.[59] Shortly afterwards, the US White House released details on what the 'Build Back Better World' (B3W) partnership would like, though one must be careful not to confuse this initiative with the similarly titled 'Build Back Better Framework' that President Biden has launched as an internal investment programme in the US.[60] The B3W is aimed at addressing an identified $40 trillion funding gap for the developing world and focuses on four particular areas: climate, health and health security, digital technology, and gender equity and equality.[61] The US said that its usual developmental tools will be deployed (e.g. USAID and EXIM) but that it 'hopes' that private capital and other G7 partners will contribute to 'collectively catalysing hundreds of billions of dollars of infrastructure investment for low- and middle-income countries in the coming years'. This lack of detail – no exact financial commitment nor timeline has been offered – has been identified and criticised by onlookers,[62] with Crabtree noting that all that has been announced is that there will be a G7 taskforce set up to implement the B3W.[63]

The White House, however, does provide details on its 'guiding principles', which are very similar to the EU's expressions of its principles when dealing with the rest of the world. They are that the B3W will be:

- Values-driven: Infrastructure development carried out in a transparent and sustainable manner – financially, environmentally, and socially – will lead to a better outcome for recipient countries and communities. We will offer countries a positive vision and a sustainable, transparent source of financing to meet their infrastructure needs.
- Good governance and strong standards: High standards have become ever more important at a time when governments are grappling with complex decisions on how to tackle climate change, build back local economies, direct scarce financing, and boost employment in an inclusive way. We are committed to providing citizens of recipient communities with the long-run benefits they expect and deserve from infrastructure projects. Our efforts will be guided by high standards and principles, such as those promoted by the updated Blue Dot Network, relating to the environment and climate, labour and social safeguards, transparency, financing, construction, anti-corruption, and other areas.
- Climate-friendly: The investments will be made in a manner consistent with achieving the goals of the Paris Climate Agreement.
- Strong strategic partnerships: Infrastructure that is developed in partnership with those whom it benefits will last longer and generate more development impact. Infrastructure created under the B3W will be developed through consultation with communities and assessing local needs as true partners. We will establish a task force together as a G7, and with others, to coordinate, harmonize our efforts, and increase our impact and reach.
- Mobilise private capital through development finance: Status quo funding and financing approaches are inadequate to address the tremendous infrastructure gap in low- and middle-income countries. We are committed to augmenting the development finance tools at our disposal to support and catalyse a significant increase in private capital to address infrastructure

needs. Infrastructure investment by a responsible and market-driven private sector, paired with high standards and transparency in public funding, is crucial for long-run development effectiveness and sustainability.

- Enhancing the impact of multilateral public finance: Multilateral development banks and other international financial institutions (IFIs) have developed rigorous standards for project planning, implementation, social and environmental safeguards, and analytical capability. The United States will incorporate these standards and safeguards to help ensure that US taxpayer resources are used appropriately and effectively. We will work with the IFIs to enhance their catalytic impact and increase the mobilisation of capital – both public and private – needed for impactful and sustainable infrastructure investment.[64]

At least there is more sentiment displayed here regarding partnership than in other initiatives, but the conditionality is still clear and will be read accordingly. It is abundantly clear that the B3W has been designed to counter the BRI, and its focus on areas where the BRI is the weakest makes sense.[65] However, there are inherent issues within the construction and idea of the B3W that many are predicting could be crippling to its chances of succeeding.

Leaving aside the fact that no new money is being committed to this project, it is also the case that even amongst G7 members, there is a clear lack of unity. Whilst the UK willingly and has traditionally followed the US' lead, European members of the G7 are not so inclined to do so given their trading links with China; Italy, as a good example, is part of the BRI and has been since 2019,[66] although that relationship has been hounded by US pressure and internal political strife in Italy.[67] We are seeing similar disunity within the G7 at the time of writing as Germany and others refuse to support all of the US' decisions taken against Russia because of its aggression towards Ukraine.[68] However, perhaps the biggest issue for the B3W is the need to bring private capital on board to achieve its aims.

Goodman and Hillman make the correct point that public investment cannot meet the needs of the developing world alone. To do that, private investment and the capacity it has will need to be unlocked.[69] This need is not new and has been understood for a long time and has been referred to as the 'technocratic holy grail' of infrastructure development.[70] The issue is not liquidity, but risk aversion. Whilst there are plenty of resources available for investment, private capital has traditionally baulked at the idea of investing in arenas that are traditionally lowly rated and understood to have inherent issues such as poor governance, a weak rule of law, and have many instances recorded of poor private-public partnerships. To resolve this issue, two solutions have been put forward. The first is something that does take place more often than not, which is where a government will build infrastructure but sell it to a private provider to manage and maintain. The other, which is being promoted by the IMF, is that 'governments could help to "crowd in" private finance by, among other things, mitigating risks at the start of a project and offering compensation if things go wrong at the end'.[71] Essentially, what is being called for is a level of insurance to entice private actors into the arena. Whether this is possible or something that could be provided and accepted by private actors is another matter entirely.

Essentially, what lies ahead for the B3W is a 'daunting road'.[72] Crabtree suggests it is daunting because infrastructure is expensive, there is not much private appetite for engaging with the risk that such endeavours naturally bring, and there is a clear lack of unity among G7 partners regarding foreign policies. In addition, initiatives such as the Global Gateway stand to dilute the challenge to the BRI, not strengthen it. Ultimately, and to repeat, it is potentially a question of authority and coordination, two elements which the West are witnessing decreasing levels of on the global stage. It is far too early to say that the global power pendulum has moved irrevocably away from the West, but it is certainly moving. The reactionary, scrambled, and superficial nature of the US and EU's responses to the BRI shows a weakness that is being understood on the global stage and because of that, the B3W's success or failure is hugely significant, perhaps more than its originators have bargained for.

6.5 Conclusion

The title to this chapter was, perhaps, intentionally misleading. It was never my intention to present to you a 'future' of the continent because, quite clearly, that is not possible. How this geo-political squabbling will play out on the continent is anybody's guess. What is abundantly clear to see though is that Africa continues to be at the centre of the world on many levels.

On a purely academic level, it is fascinating to see how the continent is being exposed to a variety of ideologies that are pulling at the continent's seams. The traditional colonial model of the French, the militaristic approach of the Americans, and the economic approach of the Chinese offer very different futures for those on the continent. The reality is that Africa, as a continent, will be shaped by all three because each country will have its uses for each of the approaches. Despite the claims of cooperating with Africa or claims of seeking to improve democracy on the continent, or providing for a privileged position with an elite European country, African countries will likely attempt to do what works for *them* best, as they should.

However, the analysis in the chapter puts other elements into very different lights. The hypocrisy of the American-controlled multilateral institutions demanding that vulnerable countries implement democratic standards whilst America is the largest seller of Arms to the continent is appalling. The hypocrisy of the Chinese claiming to be anti-interventionist whilst selling nearly as much military equipment to the continent and developing secret deals to extract the natural resources the ever-growing Chinese economy needs is just as appalling. Finally, the French approach of demanding that vulnerable countries establish an internal process that encourages liberty whilst corruptly extracting natural resources and propping up some of the worst criminals *in human history* is equally as appalling. These instances provide us with fantastic lenses with which we can analyse the continent much better, but be under no illusion – they are the most tragic of lenses.

Notes

1 Sahr John Kpundeh, *Democratization in Africa: African Views, African Voices* (The National Academies of Sciences, Engineering, Medicine 1992) 32.
2 Robert Mattes and Michael Bratton, 'Do Africans Still Want Democracy? This New Report Gives a Qualified Yes' (2016) *Washington Post* (Nov 25) www.washingtonpost.com/news/monkey-cage/wp/2016/11/25/do-africans-still-want-democracy-this-new-report-gives-a-qualified-yes/.
3 Larry Diamond, 'Facing Up to the Democratic Recession' (2015) 26 *Journal of Democracy* 1 141–155.
4 Andrew Sayer, *Why We Can't Afford the Rich* (Policy Press 2015).
5 Nic Cheeseman, 'Both Democracy and Authoritarianism Are on the Rise in Africa' (2019) *The Conversation* (Feb 18) https://theconversation.com/both-democracy-and-authoritarianism-are-on-the-rise-in-africa-111789.
6 Ibid.
7 Ibid.
8 John Mukum Mbaku, 'Threats to Democracy in Africa: The Rise of the Constitutional Coup' (2020) *Brookings Institute* (Oct 30) www.brookings.edu/blog/africa-in-focus/2020/10/30/threats-to-democracy-in-africa-the-rise-of-the-constitutional-coup/.
9 Neil Munshi, 'Democracy Erodes in Central and West Africa' (2021) *Financial Times* (Mar 7) www.ft.com/content/d7319cb8-48c3-4acf-bfcf-7aaae0e5f9fd.
10 Ibid.
11 Nic Cheeseman, 'How Western Companies Undermine African Democracy' (2020) *The Africa Report* (Nov 16) www.theafricareport.com/50500/how-western-companies-undermine-african-democracy/.
12 David Pilling, 'Democracy in Africa is in Retreat' (2020) *Financial Times* (Dec 23) www.ft.com/content/ce3626cb-a8e7-4663-a93b-478be992fe78.
13 Akin Iwilade, 'Has the Rise of China in Africa Made Democratisation Less Likely?' (2014) 1 *Accord: Conflict Trends*. www.accord.org.za/publication/conflict-trends-2014-1/ 3.
14 Yike Fu, 'The Quiet China-Africa Revolution: Chinese Investment' (2021) *The Diplomat* (Nov 22) https://thediplomat.com/2021/11/the-quiet-china-africa-revolution-chinese-investment/#:~:text=Over%20the%20same%20period%2C%20Chinese,the%20United%20States%20since%202014.
15 Iwilade (n 13).
16 Ibid.
17 Ibid.
18 Yun Sun, 'An Examination of the 2035 Vision for China-Africa Cooperation' (2021) *Brookings* (Dec 27) www.brookings.edu/blog/africa-in-focus/2021/12/27/an-examination-of-the-2035-vision-for-china-africa-cooperation/.
19 Eric Schewe, 'Why is the U.S. Military Occupying Bases Across Africa?' (2018) *JSTOR Daily* (Apr 11) https://daily.jstor.org/why-is-the-u-s-military-occupying-bases-across-africa/.
20 Iwilade (n 13).
21 Schewe (n 19).
22 Nick Turse, 'Pentagon's Own Map of US Bases in Africa Contradicts Its Claim of "Light" Footprint' (2020) *The Intercept* (Feb 27) https://theintercept.com/2020/02/27/africa-us-military-bases-africom/.
23 Judd Devermont, 'Defending the U.S. Military Presence in Africa for Reasons beyond Counterterrorism' (2020) *Center for Strategic & International Studies* (May 19) www.csis.org/analysis/defending-us-military-presence-africa-reasons-beyond-counterterrorism.
24 Theo Neethling, 'Why Foreign Countries are Scrambling to Set Up Bases in Africa' (2020) *The Conversation* (Sept 15) https://theconversation.com/why-foreign-countries-are-scrambling-to-set-up-bases-in-africa-146032.

25 Horace G. Campbell, 'The United States and Security in Africa: The Impact of the Military Management of the International System' (2017) 42 *Africa Development* 3 45–71, 58.
26 Ibid 57.
27 Ibid.
28 Ibid 60 onwards in particular.
29 Devermont (n 23).
30 Nikolay A. Medushevskiy and Alisa E. Shishkina, 'Modern French Policy on the African Continent: Transformations of a Francafrique Model' (2021) *Journal of Asian and African Studies* 1–17, 2.
31 Ibid 5.
32 Emma Farge, 'Echoes of "Francafrique" Haunt Central African Democracy' (2015) *Reuters* (Nov 12) www.reuters.com/article/us-africa-france-idUSKCN0T02LD20151112.
33 Paul Melly and Vincent Darracq, 'A New Way to Engage? French Policy in Africa from Sarkozy to Hollande' (2013) *Chatham House* (May) www.chathamhouse.org/sites/default/files/public/Research/Africa/0513pp_franceafrica.pdf.
34 Ibid.
35 Paul-Simon Handy and Felicite Djilo, 'Françafrique Is a Blunt Tool for Explaining Foreign Policy' (2021) *Institute for Security Studies* (Oct 13) https://issafrica.org/iss-today/francafrique-is-a-blunt-tool-for-explaining-foreign-policy.
36 Victor Mallet, Neil Munshi, and David Pilling, 'Why Macron's Attempt to Reset French Ties to Africa Has Hit Trouble' (2020) *Financial Times* (Oct 27) www.ft.com/content/cea9cdd9-c500-41bc-a2ae-2e4c01eaf2e8.
37 Medushevskiy and Shishkina (n 30) 11.
38 European Commission, 'Global Gateway: Up to €300 Billion for the European Union's Strategy to Boost Sustainable Links around the World' (2021) https://ec.europa.eu/commission/presscorner/detail/en/ip_21_6433.
39 Andrea Moreschi, *The Case for a "Links, Not Dependencies" Approach to EU Engagement in the Indo-Pacific* (Observer Research Foundation Issue 519, 2022) 3.
40 European Commission (n 38).
41 European Commission, *Global Gateway* (2022) https://ec.europa.eu/info/strategy/priorities-2019-2024/stronger-europe-world/global-gateway_en.
42 Kenzo Tribouillard, 'Global Gateway: Positioning Europe for a Sustainable Future: Three Questions to Maaike Okano-Heijmans' (2022) *Institut Montaigne* (Feb 22) www.institutmontaigne.org/en/blog/global-gateway-positioning-europe-sustainable-future.
43 Benedikt Erforth and Kerstin Fritzche, 'Towards a Digital Development Partnership that Meets African Interests' (2022) *Heinrich Boll Stiftung* (Jan) 16.
44 Moreschi (n 39).
45 Alfonso Medinilla, Katja Sergejeff, and Ennatu Domingo, 'The Geopolitics of African Renewable Energy: European and Chinese Investments in a Global Green Transition' (2022) 316 *ECDPM* (Jan) https://ecdpm.org/wp-content/uploads/Geopolitics-African-renewable-energy-ECDPM-Discussion-Paper-316-2022.pdf 1.
46 Ibid 21.
47 Ibid 24.
48 Yew Lun Tian, 'China Willing to Work with US on Build Back Better World Initiative' (2022) *Reuters* (Feb 28) www.reuters.com/world/china/china-willing-work-with-us-build-back-better-world-initiative-2022-02-28/.
49 Ibid.
50 Frederick Kliem, 'Europe's Global Gateway: Complementing or Competing with BRI?' (2021) *The Diplomat* (Dec 7) https://thediplomat.com/2021/12/europes-global-gateway-complementing-or-competing-with-bri/.
51 Medinilla et al. (n 45) 6.
52 Kliem (n 50).
53 Medinilla et al. (n 45) 6.
54 Tribouillard (n 42).

55 Matthew P. Goodman and Jonathan E. Hillman, 'The G7's New Global Infrastructure Initiative' (2021) *Center for Strategic & International Studies* (June 15) www.csis.org/analysis/g7s-new-global-infrastructure-initiative.
56 Tribouillard (n 42).
57 Goodman and Hillman (n 55).
58 G7, *Carbis Bay G7 Summit Communique* (2021) www.g7uk.org/wp-content/uploads/2021/06/Carbis-Bay-G7-Summit-Communique-PDF-430KB-25-pages-5.pdf.
59 Ibid.
60 The White House, *The Build Back Better Framework: President Biden's Plan to Rebuild the Middle Class* (2021) www.whitehouse.gov/build-back-better/.
61 The White House, 'Fact Sheet: President Biden and G7 Leaders Launch Build Back Better World (B3W) Partnership' (2021) www.whitehouse.gov/briefing-room/statements-releases/2021/06/12/fact-sheet-president-biden-and-g7-leaders-launch-build-back-better-world-b3w-partnership/.
62 Goodman and Hillman (n 55)
63 James Crabtree, 'Competing with the BRI: The West's Uphill Task' (2021) 63 *Survival* 4 81–88.
64 The White House (n 61).
65 Pradumna B. Rana, 'G7'S "Build Back Better World": Rival to China's BRI?' (2021) 109 *RSIS Commentary* (July 14) www.think-asia.org/bitstream/handle/11540/13896/CO21109.pdf?sequence=1.
66 Ibid.
67 Francesca Ghiretti, 'The Belt and Road in Italy: 2 Years Later' (2021) *The Diplomat* (Mar 23) https://thediplomat.com/2021/03/the-belt-and-road-in-italy-2-years-later/.
68 Martin Farrer, 'Russia Threatens Europe's Gas Supplies as West Mulls Oil Import Ban over Ukraine Invasion' (2022) *The Guardian* (Mar 8) www.theguardian.com/world/2022/mar/08/russia-threatens-europes-gas-supplies-as-west-mulls-oil-import-ban-over-ukraine-invasion.
69 Goodman and Hillman (n 62).
70 Crabtree (n 63) 84.
71 Ibid 86.
72 Ibid 88.

Conclusion

This book has endeavoured to introduce you to and then provide a solution for the credit rating impasse. The financial situation affecting the world's most vulnerable countries is bleeding into their ability to protect their own citizens. In this book, we focused on African countries because of their overrepresentation in the multilateral debt treatment initiatives developed by the G20 and administered by the IMF. However, whilst the book's narrative displays the current situation's place in a much longer story of the continent's relationship with the rest of the world, the impasse affects the most vulnerable irrespective of where they are. The need to get to some sort of a resolution is evidently acute.

Business as usual has been put forward by some to alleviate the problem. The sad truth is that their observations are quite astute as the immediate pain would be relieved should the countries decide to default on their obligations. However, this book is of the mind that longer-term solutions can be implemented now to provide relief immediately and a more progressive system moving into the future. The lack of a bankruptcy mechanism on the global scene is perhaps the fault of the global elite, but there exists an opportunity to make slight adjustments to the financial architecture that can provide, essentially, a similar (but admittedly lesser) effect. In the corporate world, debtors can usually restructure their debt obligations with their creditors, and it is usually encouraged in the face of financial trouble, but on the sovereign scene it is considered to be too problematic.

By linking the need to break the impasse with the need to build solid fundamentals in a part of the world that has never had the chance, the opportunity ahead of the global community is great. Collaboration, in the truest sense of the word, is now required. Leading legislative bodies need to take bold steps in recalibrating their regulatory strategies towards the rating agencies to allow them to be more flexible. Creditors need to be true to their word and want to engage with their distressed debtors. Rating agencies need to strive to be more than just gatekeepers extracting economic rent from their position. Sovereign debtors need to engage with the theoretical role they play in the capital markets and embark on significant programmes of increased transparency and disclosure. Competing governments on the global scene need to allow Africa to grow, rather than impeding its growth for their own ends.

DOI: 10.4324/9781003261223-8

That is a lot of 'need'. The reality of the situation, however, is very different. Africa, as a continent, has a long and painful relationship with the rest of the world in the modern era. The continent that gave the world leading civilisations was reduced to the playground of the powerful, and it felt the consequences. Extractive policies, merged with brutal disregard for human life, have been the modern history of the continent, and all that has changed is the approach. Modern Africa continues to sit in the middle of geo-political tussles and, therefore, the will to help the continent truly and sustainably develop seems to be lacking across the board.

How to fix that situation is another question entirely, and presumably, every effort would be nothing short of academic. It appears that there is a simple equation when it comes to Africa's place on the global stage: it has precious natural resources, and much larger players need them. That is the unfortunate truth. With that being the case, what use would it be to implement the aspects presented here in this book? Of course, breaking the credit rating impasse will not alter that underlying dynamic affecting the continent, but it can positively change the experience of the African economies moving forward. The rise in the usage of the capital markets is, I argue, irrevocable. If that is the case, then consistently applying pressure to make the dynamics of that relationship fairer for debtors, anywhere in the world, is important. By altering the credit rating dynamic that is so key for the debtor–creditor relationship, there is a chance to build a new and progressive framework. It should not be the case that countries *cannot* renegotiate their debts with creditors.

Focusing on the credit rating agencies for a moment, this opportunity is important. For too long, credit rating agencies have been rightly identified as a troublesome industry. Entrenched conflicts of interest, malfeasance, a profit-only culture, and actively participating against the investor they are supposed to protect are just some of the issues that have been accurately identified. For once, however, the criticism being levelled at the credit rating agencies in this instance is, for many reasons, unfair. There have been instances where credit rating agencies could have communicated better, but the ultimate story is that if they did not raise these concerns about creditworthiness in the face of potential restructurings, they would be widely liable according to the laws set by the governments that make up the G20. For the G20 countries and the multilateral institutions to blame the credit rating agencies as they have been doing is irresponsible at best. Whilst it is not comfortable for me, as a researcher of the credit rating agencies for many years, to deflect blame away from the credit rating agencies, on this occasion, it is arguably necessary. The campaign of information regarding the reasons why countries should not default is, indeed, often worrying. However, whilst credit rating agencies are part of the IIF and stand to lose out if countries default, the private creditors must shoulder much more blame than they have had to for this. The performance of the IIF has been nothing short of scandalous, with its backtracking and lack of concern for the debtor which, even on a basic level, is short-sighted. Yet, this is strangely a fantastic opportunity for the credit rating agencies.

On the back of criticism, there stands an opportunity now to be a force for good and remain profitable. To incorporate a system that promotes good financial behaviour from sovereigns and ultimately builds a better global community in the face of species-threatening concerns would turn the tables for the credit rating agencies. It would also bring many more countries into the fold, meaning increased business in the sovereign sector. The one element that I must declare here is that this plan places a lot of trust in an industry for which I have very little trust. There would be nothing, for example, to stop the credit rating agencies from simply saying 'no' to any potential implementation. One can imagine claims of 'we still may be liable' (perhaps through civil litigation) or 'we do not want interference in our processes' coming from the agencies (or, even more than imagine, perhaps anticipate). However, there is a binding force on the global scene, and that is legislation. The EU were an early adopter of stringent regulation in the credit rating sector, and it has led to results. More is now needed from the same sources of change.

To return to the start of this conclusion, only a truly collaborative effort will suffice. The roles of civil society, private and official creditors, credit rating agencies, and sovereign debtors will have to coalesce to break what is a global problem that has been repeated far too often. The once-in-a-century global pandemic is imposing a tragic toll on the world, both developed and developing, and the only hope moving forward is that the painful cloud has a silver lining in it.

Index